N K. SCOTT

ks
Ever Spoken
ho Ever Lived
Notebook

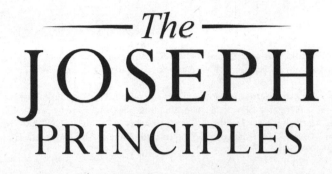

The
JOSEPH
PRINCIPLES

*Turning Adversity and Heartache
into Miraculous Living*

STEVEN K. SCOTT

W PUBLISHING GROUP

AN IMPRINT OF THOMAS NELSON

Published in Nashville, Tennessee, by W Publishing, an imprint of Thomas Nelson.

Thomas Nelson titles may be purchased in bulk for educational, business, fundraising, or sales promotional use. For information, please email SpecialMarkets@ThomasNelson.com.

Unless otherwise noted, Scripture quotations are taken from The Holy Bible, New International Version`, NIV`. Copyright © 1973, 1978, 1984, 2011 by Biblica, Inc.` Used by permission of Zondervan. All rights reserved worldwide. www.Zondervan.com. The "NIV" and "New International Version" are trademarks registered in the United States Patent and Trademark Office by Biblica, Inc.`

Scripture quotations marked as BSB are taken from The Holy Bible, Berean Study Bible, BSB. Copyright © 2016, 2018 by Bible Hub. Used by permission. All rights reserved worldwide.

Scripture quotations marked ESV are taken from the ESV` Bible (The Holy Bible, English Standard Version`). Copyright © 2001 by Crossway, a publishing ministry of Good News Publishers. Used by permission. All rights reserved.

Scripture quotations marked KJV are taken from the King James Version. Public domain.

Scripture quotations marked NASB are taken from the New American Standard Bible` (NASB). Copyright © 1960, 1962, 1963, 1968, 1971, 1972, 1973, 1975, 1977, 1995, 2020 by The Lockman Foundation. Used by permission. www.lockman.org

Scripture quotations marked NKJV are taken from the New King James Version`. Copyright © 1982 by Thomas Nelson. Used by permission. All rights reserved.

Scripture quotations marked NLT are taken from the Holy Bible, New Living Translation. © 1996, 2004, 2015 by Tyndale House Foundation. Used by permission of Tyndale House Ministries, Carol Stream, Illinois 60188. All rights reserved.

Any internet addresses, phone numbers, or company or product information printed in this book are offered as a resource and are not intended in any way to be or to imply an endorsement by Thomas Nelson, nor does Thomas Nelson vouch for the existence, content, or services of these sites, phone numbers, companies, or products beyond the life of this book.

ISBN 978-0-7852-9155-8 (audiobook)
ISBN 978-0-7852-9154-1 (eBook)
ISBN 978-0-7852-9152-7 (HC)

Library of Congress Control Number: 2021950979

Printed in the United States of America
22 23 24 25 26   LSC   10 9 8 7 6 5 4 3 2 1

To my best friend.

Lord Jesus, You fill my days with Your inexhaustible mercy and grace. Every day I wake up astonished by Your words and amazed by Your love. Though I have turned my back on You so many times, You have never turned Your back on me. You have never left me or forsaken me. You truly are a friend who sticks closer than a brother. There is none like You!

CONTENTS

CONTENTS

INTRODUCTION

You Don't Have to Keep Hurting

So when the Midianite merchants came by, his
brothers pulled Joseph up out of the cistern
and sold him for twenty shekels of silver to
the Ishmaelites, who took him to Egypt.

Genesis 37:28

Joseph was only seventeen when his world came crashing down. His own brothers threw him into a well and left him for dead. Then they had a change of heart when they happened to see a caravan of merchants headed toward Egypt. They decided that instead of leaving him for dead, they would retrieve him from the well and sell him into slavery. In a matter of minutes, Joseph went from being the most cherished son of his father to becoming a slave transported to a foreign country. Everyone he loved was ripped from him in an instant. He lost all of his privileges and rights; he lost his beloved family, his friends, and everything he valued;

all of his hopes and dreams were stolen. The only future he could see was that of being a slave.

Later, after becoming a trusted servant and manager of his owner's estate, he was thrown into prison for refusing temptation and instead choosing to honor his owner and honor his God. Yet, despite his terrible circumstances, he became the most revered and highest-ranking individual in Pharaoh's empire. His actions saved two nations from starvation.

How could this happen to someone whose whole life had been stolen and whose future had been trashed? The answer can be found in his intimate and unique relationship with God. As we look at his life, we discover twelve principles that governed his attitudes and actions. Yet his recorded words were so sparse, we do not receive any teaching from him that shows us *how* we can apply those principles to our lives. His story leaves us clueless about how we can experience the same miraculous transformations that he experienced.

That's the bad news. The good news is that about sixteen hundred years later, Jesus Christ revealed the precise steps of action that would enable us to experience the miraculous transformation and unimaginable outcomes Joseph experienced—and an even greater level of intimacy with God. In the lives of both Joseph and Jesus, we see amazing revelations and specific steps we can quickly take to overcome our hurts, our past traumas, and even our most heartbreaking experiences—whether they happened today, yesterday, or even a lifetime ago.

"That's terrible!"
    "How awful!"
    "I am so sorry!"
    "What a horrific accident."
    "How could he do that to you?"
    "Cruel."
    "Hateful."

"Just plain evil."

These are expressions we hear, say, or feel many times throughout our lives. They describe events and experiences that create sadness, discouragement, despair, and even desperation. They can rob us of all hope for recovery and happiness. They often erode or even destroy one's faith in God, raising the question, "How could a loving God allow such a terrible thing to happen?"

Changes in relationships can create heartaches that may range from unsettling and jarring to life altering or even life shattering. Losing a relationship to substance abuse, addiction, divorce, or death is so common that most of us have experienced some of these losses at one time or another. For many, it may seem like a day doesn't go by without hearing of someone we love going through a terrible trial. Even changes in our jobs or careers can cause frustration, fear, depression, despair, and of course anger and bitterness. The COVID-19 pandemic alone multiplied tragic situations by millions throughout the world. It wasn't just the millions who died or the hundreds of millions who were infected. The number of people who lost jobs, the businesses that failed, and the lives and families that were negatively affected or even shattered is incalculable. These people who thought they were sailing along on smooth seas with no storms in sight were capsized by this cruel and indiscriminate COVID-19 storm without a life jacket to save them from their perilous fate.

And then there are those trials that cause the greatest levels of pain—the agony of watching those we love experience severe illness, injury, or death. Many of my dearest friends have suffered through the chronic illness and death of a parent, a sibling, a spouse, or even a child. They go through pain more devastating than their worst nightmare. But unlike a nightmare, these situations and the anguish they create don't go away when people wake up the next morning.

During the past couple of years, a number of my closest friends have unexpectedly lost their middle-aged spouses to death from cancer or heart attacks. One of my dearest friend's pregnant daughter was murdered by her husband. One of my employees came home from church to find that his wonderful fifteen-year-old son had committed suicide because he was being bullied at school. Suicide is now the number two cause of death for young people between the ages of fifteen and twenty-four in every state.[1] Substance abuse and automobile accidents are the other top causes of death for young people. Psychologists tell us that the loss of a child at any age creates the worst level of grief a person can experience.[2] As I write this, I'm on a plane, and the businessman next to me just finished telling me the story of how his twenty-year-old son fell into depression and took his own life four years ago.

All of this is to say that nearly everyone you meet can tell you a story of unimaginable pain that they or someone they love has experienced.

How About You?

What trials, heartaches, and heartbreaks have you had to deal with over the past few years? Are there any you are dealing with right now? What tragedies have happened to people you know or love? How often have you or someone you loved asked the question, "Why did God let this happen?" Maybe your very belief in God has been shaken to the core. While it's impossible for me or anyone else to tell you why God has allowed any tragedy to happen to you or your loved ones, I can tell you that when you begin to apply the Joseph Principles, everything will change. You will find hidden treasures that will not only change your view of those tragedies but also transform every aspect of your life. Any lost faith will be restored. Whatever faith you have will grow beyond anything you've ever imagined. You will be set free from the disappointment, the heaviness, and the brokenheartedness that may have plagued you. You will be delivered from the anger and resentment that may have taken root in your life and sabotaged your ability to be happy.

We do not use the Joseph Principles to psych ourselves up or become positive thinkers. This would provide only a shallow and temporary relief at best. It may momentarily lift us out of our doldrums, but before we know it, we will sink back down into even greater discouragement and despair. And any positive thinking can be quickly vaporized by our realities or other events that force themselves back into the top of our minds.

Specific Steps of Action That Change Everything

The Joseph Principles provide a concrete foundation on which a miraculous transformation can take place. But it doesn't stop there. In the chapters ahead you will not only come into a deeper understanding of these principles but you will also be empowered with the specific steps of action you can follow to experience these principles and their glorious benefits. Taking these steps can liberate you from the oppression and bondage brought on by the hurts you are currently enduring, no matter how small or how great they may be. As you experience this miraculous liberation and transformation, you will also become equipped to liberate others who have been oppressed and held in bondage by their hurts. If any of your family members—even your children—are dealing with trials, big or small, you will be able to help guide them step-by-step through this process. If your family knows anyone who is being bullied, these principles can be the difference between life and death.

Whenever adversity comes our way, whether light or heavy, it always has one of two effects: either it interrupts and obstructs our fellowship with God or it becomes a springboard into a more intimate relationship with Him. Sadly, for most people it interrupts or obstructs their walk with God. Knowing the Joseph Principles and applying them does just the opposite. They create a springboard that can catapult you into a transformational, daily, moment-by-moment walk with God. You can experience His presence in your days and nights at a level you may have never known.

A Process That Brings the Brokenhearted into a Deeper Level of Intimacy with God

For most people who are hurting, religion just doesn't cut it. At the time of your biggest heartbreak, you may have gone to a church service and experienced a great teaching or a wonderful worship service. But you left still feeling an ache that simply would not go away. You may have even thought, *What's wrong with me? Why doesn't anything take the pain away?* And if your pain has been inflicted by someone else, you may think, *I just can't forgive them, even though I know I should.* However, by the time you finish this book, you will discover that God Himself has performed a miracle in the depths of your soul that no religious activity was able to accomplish. Here's the good news: the greater your hurts, the greater level of intimacy you are going to experience with the Father and the Son. You are going to see and experience God the Father and the Lord Jesus Christ to a degree you may have never seen or experienced before. Jesus said that He came to heal the brokenhearted and set the captive free.

No matter where you are right now—no matter how much your heart aches, how great your discouragement, or how hopeless you may feel—Jesus has provided a means of escape. And His escape provides a miraculous means by which your sadness can be turned into joy—a joy so great that nothing on earth will be able to take it away. Paul wrote, "No temptation has overtaken you except something common to mankind; and God is faithful, so He will not allow you to be tempted beyond what you are able, but with the temptation will provide the way of escape also, so that you will be able to endure it" (1 Cor. 10:13 NASB).

For years, some of my favorite people have wanted me to write this book. Family members and friends urged me to write it. But the timing wasn't right. During my life, I have experienced many devastating heartbreaks. Each time, God has been faithful to use the Joseph Principles and their accompanying steps of action to deliver me from defeat and despair into miraculous victory and joy.

Do You Want to Be Made Well?

In chapter 5 of the Gospel of John, Jesus came across a man lying on a cushion who had been sick for thirty-eight years. Jesus asked him, "**Do you want to get well?**" (v. 6). That is a simple yes-or-no question. But instead of answering yes, the man recited his problem and frustrations. He explained that he *couldn't* get well because of *his* limitations. You see, he did not realize who Jesus was and what He could do. He didn't know he was talking to the King of kings and the Lord of lords. He didn't know he was talking to the person who could calm a stormy sea with three simple words. He didn't know that the man looking down at him could give sight to the blind, health to the sick, and even life to the dead. This man's eyes remained fixed on his problem and his physical limitations rather than focusing on Jesus and listening to *His* solution. Jesus would have been justified to simply say, "Oh, you of little faith," and walk away. But Jesus was a man of compassion. Despite the man's lack of faith, Jesus gave him a single, simple command. The man obeyed and was instantly healed.

My dear reader, Jesus asks you, "Do you want to be made well?" He's not asking you to recite your problems and your limitations that have made healing your hurts impossible. He's not asking you to figure out or propose a solution. His question simply requires a yes-or-no answer. If your answer is yes, then I promise that you, too, will experience His miraculous deliverance and transformation. My promise is not based merely on what I've discovered; it's based on the rock-solid promises of Jesus Christ. All you need to do is take the simple steps of action He prescribes—steps that you are going to discover in the chapters ahead.

So how about it? Do you want to be made well? Yes or no?

Chapter 1

FINDING HIDDEN TREASURES WHERE YOU LEAST EXPECT THEM

> But we have this treasure in jars of
> clay to show that this all-surpassing
> power is from God and not from us.
> *2 Corinthians 4:7*

Recently, a ninety-year-old woman sold her tiny home in France so she could move into an assisted-living apartment. She asked an auction company to sell any furniture and other items in her house that might be of worth. The company sold her furniture and about a hundred other items for a total of $6,000. The items that weren't sold were to be taken to a dump at the end of the week.

On a wall in her tiny kitchen, just above the hot plate, hung a small eight-by-ten-inch painting that was coated with grime from the thousands of meals she had cooked through the decades. The painting was so insignificant she couldn't even remember how she got it. Of all the people who came through her home during the auction, not one made an offer for the painting. It was bound for the dump. The auctioneer told her, "You've got to make a decision: Do you want to keep it or get rid of it?"

Her first thought was to get rid of it. It was tiny, dark, grimy, and obviously worthless. She was ready to toss it.

Then the auctioneer took a closer look at it. Underneath the grime he could see a small crowd of men focused on a central character. He told the woman, "Maybe we should have this appraised before you get rid of it. It might be worth something." She agreed, and he took it to be assessed.

When it was cleaned up and examined by a few experts, this insignificant painting destined for the dump was appraised at between $4 and $7 *million*. But even the expert appraisers underestimated its true worth. It sold at auction for nearly $27 million. Sadly, this ninety-one-year-old widow died just a few months after the auction.[1]

Think about it: for decades this woman had lived frugally because she truly believed she had to conserve what little she had. But her reality was radically different from her belief and experience. The painting she considered worthless was so valuable it could have allowed her to live a life she had never even imagined. In addition, she could have become a philanthropist and blessed the lives of many others. In fact, she could have created a legacy that would have continued blessing people for generations—if only she had known the true worth of this simple yet invaluable treasure.

Your Hidden Treasures

As you will soon discover, you, too, have many priceless treasures in your life and experiences that have never been uncovered—treasures that can mean much more to you than monetary wealth. Because you haven't seen them, you have lived your life as if they didn't exist. And because you haven't known about them, they have likely remained unseen by the people who have surrounded you. Your family and friends, the people you work with, even the people who merely cross your path have not seen the treasures that reside within you. The painting in the woman's kitchen was never valued or enjoyed by her, her relatives, her friends, or those who went through her house on the day of the auction. It sat either unnoticed or grossly undervalued by everyone who saw it. Even the professional appraisers didn't realize its true worth. In the same manner, you may have grossly undervalued yourself, and your true worth may have never been seen or appreciated by others.

Treasure Hunting: An Empowering Step in the Joseph Principles

Before we look at the Joseph Principles, I want to pass along an amazing gift that my best friend and mentor Gary Smalley gave me over forty years ago. Gary taught me a simple process to help me find hidden treasures in my life that were created by the problems, trials, and adversities I had experienced. Discovering these hidden treasures throughout my life completely changed my attitudes and the course of my life. They replaced hopelessness with hope, regret with gratefulness, sorrow with happiness, and pessimism with optimism. They even changed my daily walk with God. Gary called the process treasure hunting. I have seen its transforming power not only in my life but also in the lives of those I have counseled, taught, and influenced.

A Big Lesson from a Tiny Stone

Charcoal currently sells for about $1 a pound. According to scientists, a pound of charcoal subjected to intense heat and 725,000 pounds of pressure per square inch for about 3.3 billion years would turn into a pound of diamonds.[2] Instead of selling for $1, that pound would be worth more than $17 million. Same amount of carbon, but the charcoal that produces the diamonds has been subjected to tremendous heat and unbearable pressure. And the product of that pressure and heat is beautiful, glorious, and of great worth. Next time you decide to barbecue, take a piece of that nearly worthless charcoal and set it next to your diamond ring and look at the tremendous difference pressure and heat make. Its beauty and worth are multiplied more than a million times.

Gary told me the heat and pressure that adversity and trials produce *always* turn our blackest lumps of coal into beautiful diamonds. But nature's diamonds aren't just lying on the ground. They're usually buried deep in the earth, and miners have to dig through mud, sand, and stone to find them. They are there, just waiting to be found.

When Gary taught me this, several Bible verses took on added meaning. James told us, "Consider it pure joy, my brothers and sisters, whenever you face trials of many kinds, because you know that the testing

> **Joseph Principle #1: Seeing How Every Trial Produces Hidden Treasures**

of your faith produces perseverance. Let perseverance finish its work so that you may be mature and complete, not lacking anything" (James 1:2–4). I used to think, *How on earth can I rejoice and be happy about the trials I'm going through or those I have been through?* Now that I understand every trial produces treasures, I *can* rejoice. I know it's just a matter of time before I find the hidden treasures. Paul told us, "Give thanks in every circumstance, for this is God's will for you in Christ Jesus" (1 Thess. 5:18 BSB). Knowing that there is treasure in every trial empowers us with gratefulness, and out of that gratefulness, we *want* to thank God in every circumstance, even those that create adversity and trials.

Although I doubt that Joseph or Jesus used this method of treasure hunting their trials, it's clear by looking at their lives and listening to their words that they both experienced the life-giving benefits of finding treasures in their trials. Finding treasures in their trials produced grateful hearts, but those treasures also revealed God's amazing sovereignty in their lives. Instead of being filled with hate and vengeance, Joseph's heart was filled with gratefulness, love, and kindness. And when he told his brothers how their hateful actions toward him had been used by God to save two nations from starvation, God and His loving sovereignty were magnificently revealed and forever displayed.

The same is even truer with Jesus. We see Him revealing and displaying treasures in every trial He confronted and experienced. When the twelve-year-old Jesus was accidentally abandoned by His parents for three days, instead of panicking or becoming hysterical, angry, or resentful, we see Him treasuring His time in the temple. His parents returned upset, only to find Him intentionally grateful. At the beginning of His ministry, after fasting for forty days, we see Him glorify God by refuting Satan's temptations with glorious truths from God's Word. And at the end of His life, a few hours before His crucifixion, even though His soul was deeply troubled, He saw the "diamonds" of saving you and me from our sins and bringing incomparable glory to the Father. He announced that *this* was the very reason for His coming (John 12:27). At the very end of His terrible suffering on the cross, He revealed the greatest diamond ever produced by any trial in the history of man. He announced, "**It is finished**" (John 19:30). He had successfully completed the Father's work. He had fully paid off the incalculable debt of our sin.

No, neither Joseph nor Jesus used Gary's process of treasure hunting in their trials, but they *did* find glorious, radiant diamonds in every one of their trials. And Gary's exercise of treasure hunting will enable us to do the same.

Red Light, Yellow Light, Green Light

Timing is a critical element in the process of treasure hunting. Four weeks ago, the eighteen-year-old daughter of friends of mine was nearly killed in a car accident. She went completely through the windshield and miraculously survived. Her family will likely not be able to treasure hunt that event for months and possibly years. The time to treasure hunt a trial is *never* during or immediately following a trial. Please don't suggest this to anyone who is immersed in the severe grief that immediately surrounds a trial. A person cannot treasure hunt when they are drowning! In the case of a death, you *never* treasure hunt the death itself. Rather, when the timing is right, you may choose to treasure hunt the circumstances that *followed* the death. For example, members of a family may look back and see that they became more appreciative and loving toward one another and intentional with their time with each other in the months and years after a family member died. But the time to treasure hunt the events that follow such a tragedy may be months or even years after the death. Even then, it must be done only when a member of the family wants to do it. When a person suffers from a severe trial, recognize that there's a big red light signaling you *not* to treasure hunt at that time.

> Timing is a critical element in the process of treasure hunting.

If you approach a person with the suggestion of treasure hunting, treat the situation as though the light is yellow, signaling you to approach them gently and with caution. And if there is even a hint that this is not something they are open to, consider the light to be red. They alone can give you a green light to lead them through this process.

Treasure Hunting Your Trials

When it comes to you and your own trials, you can treasure hunt them anytime you choose, knowing that the treasures you find will have a transformational power in your life.

Gary gave me a vivid example as to how this process works. Many years ago he told me he had just had breakfast with a professional football star and his wife. They had sought his counsel for their marriage. They were distraught because their relationship was headed downhill. The wife had become melancholy and even depressed, and she didn't know why. Even though she truly loved her husband, she had lost all desire for sexual intimacy. And because neither of them had a clue as to what was happening, they were losing hope for their marriage. They were both very open and honest with Gary and didn't hold back when it came to answering his probing questions.

Gary eventually asked the wife, "Have you ever been sexually assaulted?"

As she began to answer that question, tears welled up in her eyes. "Yes. My father molested me every day, from the time I was six years old until I moved out of the house at sixteen." As she cried, her husband gently took her hand and then hugged her.

Gary quietly asked, "Where is your dad now?"

She replied, "In prison. I have forgiven him, and I even visit him occasionally."

Gary then asked what seemed to be a very strange question. "Have you ever thanked God for your dad?"

Surprised, she replied, "Of course not!"

Her husband was visibly irritated by Gary's question. What he and his wife didn't know was that her answer had revealed to Gary she had *not* truly forgiven her dad and that, in spite of her desire to forgive and move on with her life, she had hit a wall that made both forgiveness and moving on impossible.

After he explained that to her, Gary told her he was going to lead her through a brief exercise that would launch her over that wall. The bricks and mortar that made up that wall were grief, anger, frustration, sorrow, guilt, sadness, hopelessness, and fear.

She questioned, "Could a simple exercise *really* get me over such a wall?"

Gary then said, "We're not only going to get you over that wall, but we're also going to blow it up so it can never keep you from joy and happiness ever again!"

He then explained the lesson of the diamonds and his process of treasure hunting. He told her they were going to treasure hunt her horrible experience. The question-and-answer dialogue that followed went something like this:

GARY: Do you ever let your daughters go to a sleepover at
    someone else's house?

MRS. T: No! Never!

GARY: Why?

MRS. T: Because I don't want either of them to be exploited in
    any way.

GARY: What if you are good friends with the other family?

MRS. T: No! I realize that no matter how well I know a family,
    you never *really* know what a father, a son, or even another
    friend or relative of that family might do.

GARY: Do you let them spend the night with relatives?

MRS. T: No . . . but I let my daughters' girlfriends spend the night at *our* house, and I let their female cousins spend the night at our house.

GARY: Say you're at a church picnic. Do you keep your eyes on them?

MRS. T: Of course. They're never out of sight.

GARY: Wow. You are both vigilant and extremely protective of your girls. Why?

MRS. T: Because I never want them to go through what I went through . . . *ever.*

GARY: There it is! We found it.

MRS. T: What?

GARY: Our first diamond. You are a wonderfully protective and vigilant parent because of the terrible adversity you experienced with your dad. Without this treasure, your children could have already been violated. But they haven't been, and as long as they're under your protection, they never will be.

MRS. T: I never thought of it like that. That *is* a gift!

GARY: Have you ever met other women who have been exploited?

MRS. T: Yes, of course.

GARY: How did you respond to them when they told you?

MRS. T: I cried, and then I hugged them, and then I just held them.

GARY: There are two more diamonds! You've become compassionate and empathetic. In this day and age, those diamonds are becoming more and more rare. And they're true treasures because they enable you to share your love and God's love in a way that's desperately needed by the other person. What do you say to them?

MRS. T: Usually nothing. I just hold them and cry with them. Then I tell them I'm available anytime they need me.

GARY: There's another one—listening without lecturing. This is a diamond that even most professional counselors never find. So, we've already found four priceless diamonds that are yours because of the terrible things your dad did to you. These diamonds allow you to bless the lives of your children and those who are hurting in ways that most people can't. If we prayed right now, do you think you could thank the Lord for these precious gifts and the incredible value they've added to your life and to the lives of others?

MRS. T: Yes.

GARY: Could you even thank the Lord for your dad?

MRS. T: Yes.

GARY: I want you to know that forgiving your dad does *not* in any way excuse or minimize his horrible behavior or negate its required consequences. However, it *will* release him from his obligation to you and it will release *you* from the terrible consequences you have experienced because of his behavior.

She then prayed with Gary and her husband. She thanked God for revealing her newfound treasures and then, with tears of joy, thanked Him for her dad—and meant it. She even thanked God for the new forgiveness she felt in her heart toward her dad. Gary told me that when she finished praying, her eyes glistened and her smile was radiant. When Gary saw her a couple of months later, she was a whole different person. She was smiling, laughing, beaming with joy. She told him her marriage had been completely healed and her intimacy with her husband was better than ever. She said she was now volunteering at a shelter for abused women and children.

She then said, "Gary, you won't believe what happened to me last week. A six-year-old little girl came up to me and asked, 'Mrs. T, will I *ever* be happy like *you*?' Gary, can you believe it? I'm now being referred to as an example of what happy looks like, and even children are seeing it." She added, "And you wouldn't believe how many diamonds I've found in the past few weeks by treasure hunting my other problems and trials! I'm so thankful to the Lord—I have never been so filled with gratefulness."

Can This *Really* Make a Difference? Absolutely Yes!

By the time Gary Smalley taught me treasure hunting, I had experienced many heartbreaks in both my personal life and business life. Amazingly, every trial or heartbreak I treasure hunted contained priceless diamonds that gave me a grateful heart and in many cases newly found wisdom that can be a priceless treasure.

On the business side, I lost nine jobs in my first six years out of college. When I was fired from my third job, it was not only heartbreaking—it was humiliating! My boss (the vice president of marketing) had told our entire department he was going to fire me right after lunch. He called me into his office and told me to have a seat. He then sat on the corner of his desk, looked me in the eye, and emphatically said, "Steve, you are the single greatest disappointment in my *entire* career! You will *never* succeed in marketing! You have twenty minutes to clean out your desk!" That was a terrible thing to hear because I had majored in marketing in college, and now a marketing guru was telling me that I'd never succeed in my chosen field. Cleaning out my desk with everyone in the department sneaking peeks at me added to the humiliation I felt.

The worst part was coming home to tell my wife that I had lost another job. We had no savings, and somehow I was supposed to provide for my wife and my nine-month-old little girl. I had been out of college only two years, and I had just lost my third job. Little did I know I was going to lose six more jobs in the next four years. But thanks to the book of Proverbs and the practice of treasure hunting, my boss was proven wrong. I ultimately *did* succeed in marketing and did so in a very big way.

However, each time I lost a job, I was devastated. Anyone who has been the sole provider for his or her family and has been fired knows what I'm talking about. Overwhelming feelings of failure, the humiliation of being fired, the fear of not being able to find a new job and not being able to provide even the basic needs of your family are just a few of the hurts and fears you feel. As a Christian, I wondered why God wasn't answering my prayers. I couldn't succeed no matter how hard I tried. Years later, when I finally treasure hunted the hurtful failures in my career, I found not only extraordinary diamonds but an eighteen-karat gold chain that strung them all together.

> As a Christian,
> I wondered why God
> wasn't answering
> my prayers.

On job number ten, I started a little business with a partner. He invested $5,000, and I created a way to market the unique product we had acquired. I created a television commercial and a marketing campaign that within five months took our sales from nothing to a million dollars—a week. During the next thirty-five years, I created hundreds of commercials and dozens of marketing campaigns that generated billions of dollars in sales for our small partnership.

What I now know is that each of my first nine jobs gave me a particular skill set that I hadn't previously had. All nine of these skill sets would be required to succeed on job ten. Through treasure hunting I discovered that God was not being unkind by letting me fail in each job. He *was* answering my prayers, but in His timing and His way. Instead of giving the small success I was praying for on each job, He was using my failures to move me to each new job so I could gain each new skill set. And with all nine skill sets, I was ready for job number ten. In terms of sales and profits, our little company became the most productive company in America, producing more than $3 million of revenue and a million dollars of profit per employee. The failures I had considered to be disasters were in reality treasures—treasures worth more than anything I had ever prayed for.

Instead of nine little successes, God gave me one giant success that would enable my partners and me to bless the lives of millions of people. Needless to say, by the time I had treasure hunted all of my failures, I could sincerely thank God for every one of my lost jobs—even the one where I was humiliated in front of the whole department!

Here are a few of the diamonds I discovered hidden in those first nine jobs:

- **Job #1**: Taught me critical sales techniques and how to mold my sales pitch to the specific needs of my customer. It taught me how to discover other people's frame of reference and how to use silence in awkward moments.
- **Job #2**: Taught me the skill of creative persistence and how to be an effective entrepreneur.
- **Job #3**: Taught me how to write successful direct mail and newspaper ads.
- **Job #4**: Introduced me to the man who would become my business partner three years later. He would completely change the course of my life and give me the opportunity to succeed beyond anything I had ever imagined.
- **Job #5**: Taught me the best ways to conduct marketing research. It also enabled me to meet and lead thirty-five people into a life-changing relationship with Jesus Christ and disciple them for three years.

- **Job #6**: Showed me that I could do things I had never been trained to do in college. It also taught me that I needed to partner with others effectively to achieve success.
- **Job #7**: Taught me how to create successful catalogs.
- **Job #8**: Reintroduced me to the man with whom I would later create a billion-dollar business.
- **Job #9**: Taught me how to write, direct, and produce television commercials that sold products directly to consumers. I also learned how to create and manage television marketing campaigns.

In addition to the treasures I found on the business side of my life, I've also found treasures in the midst of my greatest personal tragedies. I treasure hunted my sorrows from the deaths of my father and mother and the passing of some of my best friends. Prior to my father's death, I never really empathized with my friends who lost their dads. I looked at such events logically. For example, I would think, "That's what people do—they get old and they die." Or I'd think, "They had a good life, and now it's their time to move on." No compassion or empathy existed in those statements or the attitudes they reflected. I had no idea about all the hurts and emotions a man experienced with the passing of his father.

When my dad died, everything changed. I found the diamonds of empathy and compassion. Anytime a friend would lose his father, I would reach out to him with a call, a visit, a hug, and always a listening ear. My heart would truly ache for them, knowing they were going through what I had gone through. Equally important, they knew I truly cared about them and that I was available to them 24/7.

Recently I treasure hunted my COVID-19 hospitalization and found several ten-carat diamonds. One of the treasures consisted of the insights God gave me in relation to my fellowship with Him and my activity in ministry. Another treasure chest was the outpouring of love from my family and friends that still amazes me. I am truly grateful to the Lord for what my COVID experience did for me. I also gained the treasure of being made more aware of the limited amount of time I have on this earth, and I gained a renewed sense of wanting to be and do everything God wants me to be and do with my remaining minutes, days, and weeks.

An Unexpected Blessing

Several months ago, a family visited our corporate headquarters to consider becoming a distributor of our products in Costa Rica. I mentioned that I was writing this book, and the twenty-seven-year-old son asked me if he could look at my manuscript. As he turned the pages, he came across my first draft of this chapter. He then asked if he could have a time with me where I could help him treasure hunt a recent tragedy. An hour later, we went off by ourselves and he told me that his best friend (since he was three years old) had committed suicide a few months ago. Once again, we did *not* treasure hunt his friend's death but rather treasure hunted what this young man had experienced since his friend's death. When we finished, the young man told his mother and sister what we had done and the incredible diamonds he had found.

The mother then asked me if she could have a copy of the manuscript to take back with her when they traveled home. I gave her a copy. Two weeks later, I received a letter from her telling me how treasure hunting the severe trials of her life had transformed her. For the first time, she was able to forgive the "unforgivable" acts of her father. She wept tears of joy as she told me her story. Her dad saw so much love and compassion in her demeanor as she forgave him that he asked how *he* could know the God who had given her that much love and compassion for him. He was dying, and with only a few weeks left in his life, he asked Jesus to be his Lord and Savior.

She pleaded for me to have the book translated into Spanish because she knew so many lives could be transformed. I mentioned that to my publisher, and he agreed that they would quickly have it translated into Spanish.

Now It's Your Turn

Are you ready to treasure hunt your past trials and heartaches? You might ask, "Why should I?" or "Why now?" The answer is that it is God's will that we give thanks and be thankful in every circumstance (1 Thess. 5:18, 20). For me, that was impossible until I began treasure hunting my hurts and trials. Of course, I could always mouth the words, "Thank you, Lord." But more often than not, I didn't mean it. My heart was *not* grateful. But treasure hunting can transform a heart of sorrow and regret into a heart of gratefulness and rejoicing. Treasure hunting takes a little time and effort to learn, but it's not that hard. And the more you do it, the more you'll *want* to do it.

God wants you to partner with Him in building a heart filled with gratefulness. All happiness springs from gratefulness, and it's impossible to be truly happy and joyful when you don't have a grateful heart. Likewise, it's just as impossible to be unhappy when you have a grateful heart. A grateful heart not only makes you happier but also makes others happy to be around you. Proverbs 17:22 says, "A joyful heart is good medicine, but a broken spirit dries up the bones" (NASB). Gratefulness not only makes you happier; it keeps you healthier.

These are just a few of the reasons you should build a grateful heart, and nothing builds it faster than treasure hunting. As we saw earlier, treasure hunting also enables you to forgive more easily and more sincerely those who have hurt you. It empowers you to move your life forward and upward. By the way, the purpose of treasure hunting is not to minimize a painful experience or even justify it or compensate for it. The purpose is simply to find those unique treasures that are hidden within those experiences. When it comes to you and your trials, you can treasure hunt them anytime you choose, knowing that treasures you find will have a transformational power in your life.

Are you ready? There are only four steps. First, use the following lines to make a list of some of the trials or hurtful experiences you have experienced. The first ones that come to mind should be at the top of your list and the first ones you treasure hunt. They can be as recent as yesterday or as distant as your childhood. Second, for each trial make a list of

> It's impossible to be truly happy and joyful when you don't have a grateful heart.

the positive changes you've experienced because of that trial—changes in your attitudes, behaviors, direction of your life, and so on. Third, schedule a time with your spouse, a dear friend, a sibling, a parent, or even one of your grown children, and ask them to treasure hunt that experience with you. Chances are they will be able to recognize changes in you or the direction of your life that they have seen and you may have overlooked. Finally, pray and thank God for each treasure you have listed. Then thank God for the trial or adversity that created that treasure.

Joseph Principle #1: Seeing How Every Trial Produces Hidden Treasures

Hurts and Trials I Want to Treasure Hunt

_____

_____

_____

_____

_____

_____

_____

_____

_____

_____

Treasure Hunting Your Hurts and Trials

1. Hurt or adverse situation: _____

2. What positive changes have I experienced because I went
    through that adversity?

_____

_____

_____

3. How has that experience influenced the way I treat or relate to
    others?

_____

_____

_____

4. What have been the positive changes in the direction of my life?

_____

_____

_____

5. What have been the positive impacts or changes in my attitudes (humility, compassion, empathy, gratefulness, kindness, courage, faith, perseverance, etc.)?

_____

_____

Chapter 2

EVEN IF YOU FEEL ALONE, YOU'RE NOT!

I will never desert you, nor will
I ever abandon you.
Hebrews 13:5 NASB

The moment you begin to go through a trial of any kind, it is normal to feel alone. Even if you are surrounded by others, in moments of silence, you'll likely still feel alone, believing you are truly the only one who knows and feels the unbearable ache of your pain. What makes it even worse, the people and the world around you keep going on with their normal activity as if nothing has happened. Yet you are dying inside. Nearly everyone experiences this kind of pain many times throughout their lives.

I think the first time I felt it was when I was eight years old and I had my first strikeout in Little League baseball. Then I felt it again, every time a girl broke up with me. I really felt it when I was fourteen and my dog (who had been with me my entire life) was put to sleep. Of course, with each passing year, the wounds went deeper and were harder to shake off. With each job loss and failed business came heartache, humiliation, and fear. When I was forty-six, my father died. That took me to a level of pain I had never known. Then, one of my sons was nearly killed in an explosion—deeper pain, plus agony. Eight months later, another son was diagnosed with cancer—more pain, agony, and fear.

During the past few years, death has separated me from a number of my very dear friends, including one of my two *best* friends in life. My longtime "go-to," Gary Smalley—the same friend who taught me the invaluable lesson about treasure hunting—was gone. He had been the greatest encourager I had ever known. He motivated me to write nearly every book I published. For forty-three years, he always had the answers I needed. This was a whole new kind of pain. However, as was the case with every other hurt I had known, it was only a matter of time before the Big Flip took place—and like every other time, it came with accompanying blessings and miracles. You'll learn all about the Big Flip in the next chapter. But the question we face in this chapter is, "How do we get through the initial pain of the heartache and that horrible feeling of being alone?" How do we navigate that period of heartache and loneliness that would otherwise take months or even years to get through?

Joseph Principle #2: Knowing and Experiencing the Intimate Presence of God

Joseph was seventeen when his brothers sold him into slavery. We can assume that he had a true belief in his heart that his father's God was alive and well. He believed that his dreams, and his ability to interpret those dreams, were gifts from this God he trusted and worshipped. Even though Joseph may have felt alone and abandoned by God the day his brothers sold him into slavery, he was not. The almighty God never left Joseph's side.

By the time he was purchased as a slave by the Egyptian Potiphar, Joseph knew beyond any shadow of a doubt that God was with him. As he began to work for Potiphar, we are told, "The LORD was with Joseph, and he was a successful man" (Gen. 39:2 NKJV). The next verse tells us that even his Egyptian master saw that the Lord was with him because every project Joseph took on prospered. It was so extraordinary that even a heathen slave owner knew Joseph's level of success could have no other explanation—the God that Joseph proclaimed was indeed creating his supernatural level of success.

Later, having been falsely accused by Potiphar's wife, Joseph was thrown into prison (Gen. 39:20). Even then God was still with him: "But the LORD was with Joseph in the prison and showed him his faithful love" (v. 21 NLT). Although Joseph couldn't see God, he knew God was right there with him. So instead of becoming panicked or depressed, he was a model prisoner and became the warden's favorite. The warden put Joseph in charge of everything that happened in the prison, and we are told that, even there, everything he did succeeded (vv. 22–23).

> No matter how alone you may have felt throughout different times in your life . . . God has not abandoned you—ever.

You may not have experienced the kind of supernatural peace and success that Joseph did, but God has not abandoned you. No matter how alone you may have felt throughout different times in your life, or even how alone you may feel right now, God has not abandoned you—ever. Nor has He abandoned your loved ones who have suffered. How do I know that? You and I have something that Joseph never had, something infinitely superior to his dreams and interpretative gifts, something infinitely superior to anything he ever felt—or, for that matter, anything *we* have ever felt. We have the recorded words and teachings of God's eternal Son, the Lord Jesus Christ.

A Simple Prayer

In Jesus' words, you and I have everything we need to come into true intimacy with Him. And when you have true intimacy with Jesus, everything else in life, even your greatest hurts, loses its crippling power over you. But before you can move into this kind of intimacy with God, you must answer a few questions—not just from your mind and opinions but from your heart.

I would ask you to take a moment to pray. Ask God if He is real. Ask Him if Jesus is really His eternal Son. Ask Him if you truly matter to Him. Ask Him if He truly loves you. Ask Him if He is present with you at this very moment. If you are unsure about the answers to these questions, then be honest in your prayer and tell Him you are unsure—that you really *don't* know. He won't be offended.

I know when a person is hurting, praying can sometimes be difficult. If that's the case for you, then I would invite you to pray the prayer below. You can add anything you want to it. Pray each line thoughtfully and one line at a time. As you pray, you may feel something, or you may not. You may hear Him whisper answers, or you may not. What's important right now is simply that you are honest and transparent.

God, are You real?
Are You here with me right now?
Is Jesus really Your eternal Son?
God, do I really matter to You?

Do You really love me?
I want to know if You are real.
I want to know if Jesus is really Your Son.
I want to know if You are really present with me right now.
God, in the hours and days ahead, I want to know all of this.
And if all of this is true, please give me the faith to believe and follow Your Son.
God, I do want to know You intimately.
Amen.

You may need to read that prayer only once, or you may need to read or pray it a number of times. But I promise, if you really want to know the truth, God Himself will reveal it to you as you continue reading this book. He will give you a heart that believes and the desire and courage to follow His Son. As Jesus Himself promised to you, **"Ask and it will be given to you; seek and you will find; knock and the door will be opened to you. For everyone who asks receives; the one who seeks finds; and to the one who knocks, the door will be opened"** (Matt. 7:7–8).

> He will give you a heart that believes and the desire and courage to follow His Son.

Those are amazing promises: if you ask, seek, and knock, you will receive, you will find, and the door will be opened to you. Jesus makes these promises to anyone who will simply ask, seek, and knock. And then He makes another promise and an amazing revelation. He said, **"Which of you, if your son asks for bread, will give him a stone? Or if he asks for a fish, will give him a snake? If you, then, though you are evil, know how to give good gifts to your children, how much more will your Father in heaven give good gifts to those who ask him!"** (Matt. 7:9–11). His amazing revelation is that God wants to give good gifts to you. He loves you more than your earthly parents and even more than you love yourself.

Knowing this is what He has promised, perhaps you would like to pray that simple prayer again. As you will discover in this book (if you haven't discovered it before now), Jesus' words give us a lot more than just information and truth. He said, **"The words I have spoken to you are spirit and they are life"** (John 6:63 BSB). So they literally have the power to infuse His Spirit into *our* spirits and His life into *our* lives. They reach a place in our hearts that no other words can reach. That's why Jesus said, **"If you abide in My word, you are My disciples indeed. And you shall know the truth, and the truth shall make you free"** (John 8:31–32 NKJV). His words can set the captives free and lift those in despair out of a pit of deep oppression. If you don't believe that now, don't fret, you will by the end of this book.

Jesus' Promises to You

Did you know that Jesus made more than eighty promises to His followers? If you choose to follow Him, all of those promises are made to you. Most are conditional promises. He gives a simple condition or step of faith for you to take, and then He promises that a certain benefit will follow. For example, looking again at John 8:31–32, the promises of discipleship, knowledge of the truth, and being liberated or set free follow one simple condition: **"If you abide in My word."** Abiding in His word means that you thoughtfully read what Jesus said and then apply what He said to your daily attitudes and behavior. If a current or former adverse situation is continuing to hurt or burden you, Jesus' promise here is that as you hear and do what He says, you will be set free from that hurt and the burden that weighs you down.

For example, are you currently feeling alone? Jesus promised, **"I will** never leave you nor forsake you" (Heb. 13:5 NKJV). He also promised, "**Whoever comes to me I will never drive away**" (John 6:37). Are you currently hurting, overwhelmed, discouraged, or depressed? Jesus promised, "**Come to me, all you who are weary and burdened, and I will give you rest. Take my yoke upon you and learn from me, for I am gentle and humble in heart, and you will find rest for your souls. For my yoke is easy and my burden is light**" (Matt. 11:28–30). In these three passages, Jesus promises you He will never leave you or turn His back on you. He promises that when you come to Him, He will never push you away. He promises that when you're hurting, no matter how heavy the burden or how overwhelmed you are, if you will come to Him, He will ease your pain and lift your burden. He'll give you understanding as you "**learn from me**" (v. 29), and He will be gentle and humble in His handling of your problems. Unlike human counselors, Jesus is not looking at His watch and saying, "Time's up. See you next week." He's really saying, "Come on in, rest awhile. I'm going to give you all of the time, understanding, and support you need. In fact, we're going to use My strength to carry your load. Just relax, and I'll do all of the heavy lifting."

These are but a few of the more than eighty promises He makes to you. Are you going to ignore them, hear them but not believe them? Or are you going to hear them, believe them, and act on them? They are in your account; what you do with them is up to you. Learn them and act on them, and your faith will grow—and miracles follow faith.

Joseph Principle #2. Knowing and Experiencing the Intimate Presence of God

Chapter 3

THE BIG FLIP

You meant evil against me, but
God meant it for good.
Genesis 50:20 ESV

Most of us have been familiar with the story of Joseph and his brothers as long as we've been attending church. It's full of many lessons,
so it's understandable why this is a favorite among Bible teachers and
preachers. In Joseph's story we see the devastation that is created by envy
and jealousy and the hatred they produce. In Joseph we see a young man
whose belief in God was rock solid and whose character was one of truth
and integrity. We see him persecuted and even imprisoned because of his
refusal to compromise his morals. We see God use Joseph's persecution
and adversity to bring about miraculous outcomes and transformations,
not only in Joseph but in the people he influences. We see Joseph's con-
sistent walk in righteousness that his extraordinary faith produced. We

see his heartbreak over the death of his father. We see God's amazing sovereignty and Joseph's belief in that sovereignty, even to the point of having gratefulness in the midst of terrible suffering—brought about by his brothers' hateful actions and later his boss's evil wife. Finally, we see him forgive his brothers, not because they deserved it, or even because of their repentance, but because of his belief and trust in God's love and sovereignty over every aspect of his life.

Let's take a quick look at this story's crescendo, found in Genesis 50:15–21. It picks up immediately after the death of Joseph's beloved father:

> When Joseph's brothers saw that their father was dead, they said, "It may be that Joseph will hate us and pay us back for all the evil that we did to him." So they sent a message to Joseph, saying, "Your father gave this command before he died: 'Say to Joseph, "Please forgive the transgression of your brothers and their sin, because they did evil to you."' And now, please forgive the transgression of the servants of the God of your father." Joseph wept when they spoke to him. His brothers also came and fell down before him and said, "Behold, we are your servants." But Joseph said to them, "Do not fear, for am I in the place of God? As for you, you meant evil against me, but God meant it for good, to bring it about that many people should be kept alive, as they are today. So do not fear; I will provide for you and your little ones." Thus he comforted them and spoke kindly to them. (ESV)

The cornerstone of the Joseph Principles is simple. It is revealed in Joseph's statement, "You meant evil against me, but God meant it for good" (v. 20 ESV). And even though most of us can easily recite this statement by heart, our attitudes and behaviors show that most of us do not believe it in our hearts. Jesus taught that our behaviors flow out of the beliefs of our hearts, not out of the opinions or purported beliefs we espouse from our minds (Matt. 15:18). That's why our behavior is often contrary to the beliefs we mentally embrace and verbally profess. Most of us say we believe in the loving sovereignty of our almighty God, but we often act as if we don't. By Jesus' definition, our actions are the expressions of what we truly believe in our hearts.

When you believe in your heart that God is truly sovereign and that He loves you more than you love yourself, you will experience a supernatural peace and joy even amid extreme adversity. You will be able to experience the miraculous power to wholly forgive the offenses of others, even when those offenses were expressions of hatred intended to severely hurt you. Like rivers of living water, this amazing peace, joy, and forgiveness will automatically flow out of a grateful heart that is created by a heart belief in the loving sovereignty of the God and Father of our Lord Jesus Christ (John 7:38). If this is *not* the case for you right now, don't fret. By the time you finish this book, it will be.

Let's break down the standout elements of Joseph's story:

1. When one's jealousy and envy are not quickly and effectively dealt with, they can rapidly grow into a hatred that dominates one's heart and produces horrific behavior that reflects the spirit of murder. While Joseph's brothers decided against their initial plan to murder Joseph, by Jesus' standard, selling him into slavery and telling their father that he had been killed by an animal reflected the same murderous spirit.

2. Their evil act of selling him into slavery did not produce a lasting anger or bitterness or a vengeful heart in Joseph. Nor did it produce a bitter or rebellious spirit toward God. At the time he was sold into slavery, Joseph's heart was still committed to God. While it would have been natural for him to have abandoned his belief in God or rebel and turn his back on Him, he did neither. He

continued to believe in the loving sovereignty of God and demonstrated his faith through his continued obedience to Him.

3. Joseph's heart was filled with compassion toward his brothers rather than hatred or vindictiveness.

4. Joseph refused to allow his brothers to bow to him, or even fear him, because he knew that he was merely a man, and judgment and acts of honor and submission needed to be reserved for God alone.

5. He believed in his heart that their terrible deed and any other evils done to him throughout his life had not happened outside of the perfect, loving, and sovereign will of God.

6. He wholly forgave them—not because they deserved it but because he believed in God and His sovereignty. Over a period of decades, he had seen the miraculous outcomes that God had brought about for him through the evil actions of his brothers—miracles that not only blessed him and his family but saved the people of Egypt and Israel from starvation.

7. Joseph's true forgiveness made it possible for him to provide acts of mercy, love, and blessing toward his brothers and their children.

8. Rather than judge, condemn, or lecture his brothers with a harsh reproof, Joseph's heart was so empowered by God's grace, he was able to comfort his brothers and speak kindly to them.

It's Not Natural

By the way, Joseph's amazing faith and the behavior it produced are *not* natural. Such responses do not flow out of our human nature or our natural inclinations. In fact, they are 180 degrees contrary to human nature and our natural responses. Someone hurts us, and our natural, instant response is the desire to hurt them back. Someone gossips and says bad things about us, and our natural response is to immediately gossip and say something bad about them. That is at the very heart of our self-centered human nature. Joseph's faith and the life and actions that flowed out of it are contrary to human nature; however, they are perfectly natural to the Holy Spirit.

In the chapters ahead you will see that the Joseph Principles perfectly illustrate the teachings of Jesus. You will also discover that Jesus gives you specific steps that will enable you to use the Joseph Principles to bring transformation to your heart. And of course, it will all be doable through God's empowering grace and the ministry of the Holy Spirit. As you take these steps revealed in the teachings of Christ, your stress will be replaced with peace, your sorrow will be replaced with an indescribable joy, your confusion will be replaced with uncanny understanding and guidance, your fears will be replaced with courage, and your doubts will be replaced with a supernatural faith. Any separation that you have felt from God will be replaced with a moment-by-moment experience of His presence. Most important, you will move into true intimacy with the Father and the Son. The Holy Spirit will have free rein in your life to produce His fruit—love, joy, peace, patience, kindness, goodness, faithfulness, gentleness, and self-control (Gal. 5:22–23).

Joseph Principle #3: Believing That God Is Sovereign and Loving and Living That Belief

The third Joseph Principle is very simple—it's gaining the faith to believe in God's glorious sovereignty and incomparable love for you, even during your trials. And you'll gain the faith you need for your attitudes and behavior to flow out of your true faith in His love and sovereignty. This is clearly reflected in Joseph's statement, "What they meant for evil, God meant for good!" (Gen. 50:20). In other words, when someone says or does something that hurts you, even if it is motivated and fueled by hatred, their evil acts will *not* have the power to subvert the will of God in your life and divert your eternal destiny. In fact, this Joseph Principle reveals that God will use even the hateful acts that are intended to hurt us to bring about His perfect will—not only for our benefit but for His glory and the glory of His kingdom.

I like to refer to one of the attributes of this principle as the Big Flip. We see this attribute in action again and again throughout the Bible. Satan, his followers, and the people they influence do something evil, then God takes that evil act and flips it, creating something good and wonderful—something that is better than anyone could have imagined. This is why Paul confidently wrote, "And we know that all things work together for good to those who love God, to those who are the called according to His purpose" (Rom. 8:28 NKJV). No evil can come to us or overtake us unless God allows it—and when He allows it, He uses it to create something extraordinary for us: a hidden treasure that we will gain either in this life or in our life to come (Matt. 13:44).

The Big Flip

In the Old Testament, we see the Big Flip in the lives of so many, including Abraham, Jacob, Moses, Job, David, Daniel, Jonah, and Esther. In the New Testament, we see it in the lives of the woman caught in the act of adultery and the woman at the well. We see it in the lives of Peter and Paul and the rest of Jesus' disciples. And of course, we see its greatest demonstration in the life of Christ. We see Him falsely accused, wrongly convicted, and horrifically executed on the cross. Surely Satan and his legions of demons rejoiced, thinking they had successfully killed the Messiah and thwarted God's plan, whatever it may have been. Then came the Big Flip. Jesus rose from the grave, and His crucifixion provided the very means by which sinful people could be delivered from the eternal condemnation and consequences of their sins. His work on the cross provided the very means by which our sins could be absorbed and absolved by the Lamb of God. And Jesus' perfect righteousness could be transferred to our account, leaving us holy and blameless before God. Paul said it this way: "God made Him who knew no sin to be sin on our behalf, so that in Him we might become the righteousness of God" (2 Cor. 5:21 BSB). The greatest evil ever perpetrated by Satan and mankind was flipped into the greatest miracle ever performed by God. That which was intended to destroy any hope of man ever being cleansed and made acceptable to God became the very tool in the hand of God to cleanse man and offer Christ's righteousness to those who would believe in Him.

> The greatest evil ever perpetrated by Satan and mankind was flipped into the greatest miracle ever performed by God.

Well, That Was Then—How About Now?

The Big Flip is performed by God as often today as it was in biblical times. In fact, it has happened with every follower of Christ that I have ever come to know. It happens to us and all around us, but sadly, we usually don't see it. And because it passes right by us without notice, we miss the miracles that so often accompany it. But once you see it in your own life and follow the guidance Jesus offers us, the resulting miracles will not only astound you but will bring eternal glory to the Lord Jesus Christ and our heavenly Father. Living in the belief of this Joseph Principle that God is sovereign and loving produces attitudes and actions that strengthen our faith in Him and increase our loving actions and attitudes toward others.

An Unwanted Child Is Born, Given Away, and Abducted

Myra Wattinger had been married and divorced but had never had a child. Her occupation was that of a hospice nurse. Forty years old, she was living in the home of an elderly man she was caring for. One night, his alcoholic son came into her room and raped her. As if that wasn't bad enough, to her dismay, she became pregnant. She went to her doctor in Houston and asked for an abortion. Believing that life is precious, he refused her, and she gave birth to a son, James, in the charity ward of a Catholic hospital. She really didn't want the child, and knew she couldn't provide for him, so she ran an ad in the local paper, and a couple was found who agreed to adopt him.

Five years later, Myra changed her mind and came to the couple's home to take James back. He has since described this as one of the most traumatic events of his life. He said he can still remember the feeling of his fingernails dragging across the hardwood floor as she pulled him out from under the bed where he was hiding. He was being ripped away from the only parents he had known. After leaving the house, they hitchhiked 175 miles to Austin. They lived in abject poverty and moved close to fifteen times in the next ten years.

As a teenager, James was headed toward a worthless, pitiful life. And then came the Big Flip. Myra offered to let James have a one-week visit with the loving adopted parents he had been ripped away from ten years earlier. When he appeared at the door of their humble home, they wept. One night, they took him to church, and he made the greatest decision of his life—he invited Jesus to be his Lord and Savior and committed his life to following Him.[1]

Not long after that, the alcoholic that had raped his mother came back into their lives. He choked Myra, and she passed out. James thought she was dead. The man then came into James's room and threatened to kill him. James grabbed his rifle and pointed it at him in self-defense. Had the man taken one more step toward him, James would have had to shoot him. Instead, the man simply swore at him, and James held him at bay until the police arrived and arrested him.[2]

Looking back, I would assume that Satan and his demons high-fived each other in delight when Myra was raped. I'm sure they also delighted in James's horrific childhood and the fact that he almost killed his biological father. But they didn't contend with the Big Flip. Within three years, eighteen-year-old James felt that God was calling him to preach. By the time he was twenty, his evangelistic crusades were citywide. His crusades began filling coliseums and stadiums. Before he transitioned to his current ministry, more than twenty million people had attended James Robison's crusades. Millions had come forward to dedicate their lives to Jesus Christ.[3]

His later ministry to the impoverished in developing countries saved the lives of more than five million people through his food programs and water-well programs. His Homes for Life programs have provided loving homes for countless orphans in numerous countries in Asia, Africa, South America, and Eastern Europe.[4] Yes, the Big Flip still happens. Once again, they meant it for evil but God meant it for good (Gen 50:20).

This is just one of countless stories that illustrate the Big Flip cornerstone of the Joseph Principles. But as inspirational as these stories may be, the question is how this incredible principle can transform your life and the lives of those you love. For me, knowing that God can perform the

Big Flip in any of my traumas and trials helps me to endure them with a degree of peace and confidence that would otherwise be elusive.

While reading this chapter, one of my sons asked me, "What about all the people that don't experience the Big Flip—who don't get rescued, like the Holocaust victims?" My answer is simple. We see only what happens in *this* life. But God's sovereignty and love extend to life after death. We know that a sparrow doesn't fall to the ground apart from His loving will, and He is truly capable of performing His sovereign love and compassion throughout eternity. For Him, righting the wrongs of others doesn't have to happen during a person's brief time on earth. He has all of eternity to perform and demonstrate the Big Flip. Jesus underscored this when He stated, **"Blessed are you when people hate you, and when they exclude you and insult you and reject your name as evil because of the Son of Man. Rejoice in that day and leap for joy, because great is your reward in heaven"** (Luke 6:22–23 BSB). Our life on earth is a grain of sand on the vast beach of God's eternity. Paul wrote, "Eye has not seen, nor ear heard, nor have entered into the heart of man the things which God has prepared for those who love Him" (1 Cor. 2:9 NKJV).

Joseph Principle #3: Believing That God Is Sovereign and Loving and Living That Belief

Chapter 4

TURNING OFF THE POWER OF YOUR WORRIES, FEARS, SORROWS, AND REGRETS

Do you not say, "There are still four months
and then comes the harvest"? Behold, I say to
you, lift up your eyes and look at the fields,
for they are already white for harvest!

John 4:35 NKJV

How often do worries and fears creep into your thoughts? If you're like most of us, it's too often. Usually a worry, fear, or stressful thought rides into our minds on the back of another thought. Or it's a reaction to a trigger that you see or hear. Sadly, it's usually only moments before they have hijacked your mind and stolen your full attention.

How often do your sorrows or regrets do the exact same thing? First, they enter your thoughts, and before you know it, they are not only controlling your thoughts but reaching into your heart and churning up feelings that hijack your emotions. Regrets and sorrows can be triggered by almost anything—a memory, a song, a fragrance, a location, or nearly anything we see or hear. They not only steal your thoughts and emotions for a few seconds; they often transport your mind and heart into distress, despair, or even depression.

I can't tell you the number of times my dear Christian friends urged me to "stop worrying." They would say things like, "The Bible tells us over and over again, 'Fear not.'" They would remind me of Jesus' commands, like, **"Don't be afraid; just believe"** (Mark 5:36). They would remind me of Paul's admonition to "not be anxious about anything" (Phil. 4:6; John 14:27). They would remind me that faith and worry are opposites and can't occupy the mind at the same time, so worry must be replaced with faith. And when I was sad or grieving, they would say things like, "Snap out of it" or "Get over it" or "Just move on." But none of them would ever tell me *how* to do any of that. Of course they would say, "Pray" or "Trust the Lord." Yes, all of their encouragements were motivated by their love for me and were truly good thoughts, but they never told me how to trust in God.

The Reset Button

Joseph had a reset button that he could activate anytime he sensed worry, fear, regret, or sorrow creeping into his mind. And as soon as he hit that button, all these burdens would instantly lose all of their power over his heart and mind. They couldn't divert his attention or blur his focus. They couldn't undermine his productivity. They couldn't even dilute his gratefulness, his love for God, or his ethics. That is how powerful his reset button was. That was a button I wanted to understand and use.

What Joseph Didn't Do, Jesus Did

Unfortunately, even though Joseph used that reset button daily, he never showed us how to use it. Jesus, however, not only revealed that button but told us exactly how to press it. In fact, He commanded us to do so anytime worries, fears, stresses, sorrows, or regrets enter our minds. But before we look at the reset button and see how to use it, let me ask you two questions:

1. What is one thing that is worrying you right now or that you have worried about anytime during the past twenty-four hours? It might be something you think about at night or something that creeps into your mind during the day. Maybe it's more than one thing; maybe you have a number of worries or fears that are confronting you regularly.
2. What is a sorrow or regret that seems to make you catch your breath or even knocks the wind out of you emotionally? Once again, if there's more than one, think about those as well.

Grab your journal, a notebook, or a sheet of paper and answer these questions. You don't need to spend a lot of time on this, but take a few minutes and jot down your responses. This is really important, so don't keep reading until you've done this. When you've finished writing, keep the paper handy and come back to this page.

All Anxieties, Worries, and Fears Come from Focusing on the Future

Now, look at what you've written down. Forgive me for stating the obvious, but every worry and fear you've written down is about something that is in the future. It might be ten minutes from now (like a phone call you're dreading), or it might be three weeks or even three months from now. But regardless of the timing, the worries and fears that create your anxiety and stress are all in the future. They are not about anything that is in your present moment.

All Sorrows, Regrets, Resentments, and Most of Your Anger Come from Focusing on the Past

Now look at the sorrows and regrets you've written down. Obviously, they all flow from events or situations in your past. Like worries and fears, they are not about anything in the present moment. I don't know about you, but every day I'm confronted by some of my regrets and sorrows. And if I don't use the reset button that Jesus commanded me to use, they quickly steal my attention and divert my focus. When that happens, if I don't quickly press this button, my mind and emotions are hijacked, and like a car going over a cliff, I quickly plunge into sadness and sometimes despair. Thankfully, since discovering this reset button, I almost never go over that cliff.

Coming into the Present Moment with God

The reset button I am talking about is one that empowers us to instantly leave the past or future thoughts on which our mind is dwelling and come into the present moment. At the moment we make that move, our worries and fears, our sorrows and regrets *instantly* lose their hypnotic and relentless grip on our mind and heart. But they can return just as fast when we leave the present moment and return our focus to the past or the future. For followers of Christ, when you are transported into the present moment, you can also transport into the presence of God. God doesn't live in the past, and He doesn't reside in the future. He dwells exclusively in the present moment.

Turning Your Moments into Miracles

A few years ago, as I was prayerfully reading the Gospel of John, God opened my eyes to this reset button. I soon discovered that it was one of the most life-changing, transformational principles and practices I had ever experienced in my relationship with Christ. It could be applied to any moment of any day of my life. It had the power to be used as one of the greatest tools of the Holy Spirit to transform my heart and daily experience. Then, as I reconsidered the story of Joseph and the Joseph Principles, I realized that this principle and the practice of applying it each day played a huge role in how Joseph was able to go on with his life after his brothers sold him into slavery.

This principle and practice not only made it possible for him to endure his trials but also was used by the Holy Spirit to empower Joseph to achieve unparalleled success. Imagine: an Israelite slave rising to the second-highest position of power in the Egyptian Empire. The principle is "Living in the present moment." The practice is learning how to instantly shift the focus of your attention from the past or the future into the moment you are in. Picture a big electromagnet suspended in the air by a crane—the type that is used in junkyards. Press the starter button to turn it on, and the moment the electric current flows into the magnet, it can easily lift a two-thousand-pound car. But the moment

> **Joseph Principle #4: Living in the Moment with God and Others**

you turn the button off, that magnet instantly loses all of its power and drops the car.

When you press Joseph's reset button to bring your mind into the present moment, you instantly turn off the power of your fears that reside in the future and the regrets that reside in your past. And like that electromagnet, they instantly lose their power, and you are set free to become fully engaged in the present moment.

You might be thinking, *What's so revolutionary about this? After all, New Age authors and motivational speakers have been talking about it for years.* If that's your response, you're partially right. In 1997 a New Age author published a book about the practice of "living in the now." *The Power of Now* by Eckhart Tolle became a worldwide bestseller, and everyone was amazed by this author's incredible insight and teaching. I can remember a friend of mine from England waving the book in my face and telling me that he had *finally* found "the answer." He was a very successful businessman who'd had major struggles with depression, and this book had given him the solution he had been looking for. "Depression is a thing of my past," he announced.

Unfortunately, within a few months he had slid back into his sea of depression. You see, it's not enough simply to know that you should live in the now; you need a power source that enables you to do it. That power source is Jesus Christ, and the electric current that delivers that power is the Holy Spirit.

Like so many truths, living in the now is a nice idea, but without the right power source, it's next to impossible to do consistently. A Harvard study published in 2010 in *Science* magazine showed that people today spend nearly 50 percent of their waking hours thinking (and living) in the past or the future.[1] Even though Eckhart Tolle was given credit as the wise revelator of this principle, the fact is Jesus proclaimed it two thousand years earlier. He not only commanded His disciples to live in the present moment but told them *how* to do it day in and day out, for the rest of their lives. Thankfully, Jesus also gave them the perfect example in the way He lived His own life every day. They witnessed Him living in the present every moment they were with Him.

Correctly Defining the Future and the Past

When I talk about the past or the future, I'm not just talking about ten years ago or five years from now. Neither is Jesus. The past is as recent as this morning or even ten minutes ago. And the future is as near as this coming weekend or an hour from now or even thinking about going to lunch in five minutes. If you are talking with a coworker and all of a sudden start wondering what's for lunch, you've drifted out of the present moment and into the future. If you're getting off the elevator and thinking, *I can't believe what my husband said this morning,* you are dwelling in the past. And instead of looking at the receptionist and showing attentive kindness, you miss the opportunity altogether because your mind isn't in the moment.

Here are some amazing realities:

- God doesn't reside in the past or the future—He lives in the present moment.
- Intimacy with God doesn't take place in the past or the future—only in the present moment.
- Miracles don't happen in the past or the future—only in the present moment.
- Love is not expressed in the past or the future—only in the present moment.

Look at all we miss when our minds or hearts are focused even one minute in the past or one minute in the future. We miss the presence of God in our present moment. We miss our ability to be intimate with Him in the present moment. We miss the opportunity to experience miracles in the present moment. We miss the chance to express our love for Him and our love for others in the present moment. All because our mind or heart is distracted and blinded by the past or future. God even defines Himself as the God of the present moment. Look at the conversation between God and Moses in Exodus 3:13–14:

> Moses said to God, "Suppose I go to the Israelites and say to them, 'The God of your fathers has sent me to you,' and they ask me, 'What is his name?' Then what shall I tell them?"
>
> God said to Moses, "I AM WHO I AM. This is what you are to say to the Israelites: 'I AM has sent me to you.'"

God called Himself I AM. Not I WAS or I WILL BE but I AM.

In Luke 9:61, a man told Jesus that he would follow Him, but first he wanted to return home and say goodbye. Jesus replied, "**No one who puts his hand to the plow and then looks back is fit for the kingdom of God**" (Luke 9:62 BSB). Jesus wasn't being harsh; He was just being truthful. He knew this man's heart was still living in the past and that he didn't want to leave his attachment behind. He also knew that the man had not gained a true vision of who Jesus was and the amazing opportunity Jesus had offered him—the opportunity to serve in the kingdom of the almighty God! Had the man had a true vision of both, He would not have even considered returning home. You don't return home to collect a strand of glass beads when someone offers you a treasure chest of diamonds. No matter what was waiting for him back home, it could not compare to the incredible joy and eternal blessing of following the King of kings and the Lord of lords in His mission. So, the man looked back and walked away while Jesus continued forward.

But there is more to the truth Jesus announced here than just that one man's situation. Just as a farmer can't effectively plow a straight furrow while he's looking back, no one whose mind or heart is looking back can experience God's presence in the moment they are in. This man was not able to experience the true realization of who Christ

> When our hearts and minds are focused on the past, we cannot experience God and all He desires for us in the moment we are in.

was and what God was offering to him because his heart and mind were focused on his past. My friend, when our hearts and minds are focused on the past, we cannot experience God and all He desires for us in the moment we are in.

But dwelling in the past isn't our only diversion from living in the moment. In the Sermon on the Mount, Jesus said, "**Therefore do not worry about tomorrow, for tomorrow will worry about itself. Each day has enough trouble of its own**" (Matt. 6:34). Moments earlier He had said, "**So do not worry, saying, 'What shall we eat?' or 'What shall we drink?' or 'What shall we wear?'**" (v. 31). "**These things dominate the thoughts of unbelievers, but your heavenly Father already knows all your needs. Seek the Kingdom of God above all else, and live righteously, and he will give you everything you need**" (vv. 32–33 NLT).

Just as Jesus told us to not set our focus on the past, here He tells us not to focus on the future—not even a day from now. Like the past, focusing on the future distracts our minds and hearts from the present moment and from hearing God and experiencing intimacy with Him.

Is It Wrong to Think About Things in the Future or Reminisce About the Past?

Does the need to live in the moment mean that we never think about the future or reminisce about the past? Absolutely not. There is nothing inherently wrong with thinking about the future or enjoying your recollections of your past. In fact, the Bible tells us frequently to be diligent, and planning for the future is a very important part of diligence. And remembering the past can bring us both joy and comfort. Many of our greatest lessons in life are learned when we look back at our past successes and failures. The people of Israel were constantly being disciplined because they did not remember the great things God had done in their past (Ps. 78:42). Every time I failed in my career, I would always revisit the failure and try to analyze what I'd done wrong. This would help me not to repeat the same mistakes in the next project.

In other words, when there is a specific purpose, it's fine to visit the past or plan for the future. However, most of the time, it's better for us and for those around us to keep our minds in the present. And whenever you are with someone else, it's critical that you bring your mind out of the past or future and into the present moment. It's also important to come fully into the moment when you need to perform a task or when you want to meditate on God's Word or have one-on-one time with God.

Had Joseph's mind and heart been stuck in the past, he never could have achieved the levels of success he did. He would have been depressed, oppressed, or even enslaved by anger, resentment, bitterness, hatred, and vindictiveness. It's impossible to build successful relationships and gain and maintain extraordinary success when such is the case. We see none of this in his relationships with his fellow slaves, his bosses, or his fellow prisoners. And we see none of this when he was finally reunited with his brothers. We see just the opposite—kindness, love, mercy, grace, charisma, and unparalleled success.

At the same time, we don't see Joseph's heart or mind continually drifting into the future. Focusing on the future would have created worry, stress, fear, entitlement, envy, and jealousy. We see none of that. And living in the past *or* the future would have robbed him of his dynamic personal relationship with God. He would not have had a moment-by-moment intimacy with God. His faith in God would have been replaced with doubt, unbelief, or even defiance. We don't see any of that in his story. Instead, we see a man who was defined by the characterization "The LORD was with him" (Gen. 39:2). Everything he was and everything that brought him purpose, joy, love, and success flowed out of a heart that was dominated by his intimacy with the Lord.

My personal revelation of experiencing the miracle of the moment came as I was reading the story of the Samaritan woman at the well in John 4. Let's take a look at what happened.

The Woman at the Well

It was nearly noon, and Jesus and His disciples had been walking in the hot desert sun since six in the morning. Jesus was tired and decided to stop and take a rest in the Samaritan town of Sychar. He sat down near a well that the Samaritans referred to as Jacob's Well. His disciples decided to travel to a nearby village to pick up food for lunch. While Jesus was seated, a Samaritan woman from another town came to the well to fill up a large pot with water and take it back to her home. Before she drew her water, Jesus asked her to give him a drink. She was shocked. Jews *never* spoke to Samaritans. In fact, they would travel long distances out of their way to avoid any contact with Samaritans. Yet this Jewish man had spoken to her, a Samaritan woman. She asked Him, "How is it that You, being a Jew, ask me for a drink since I am a Samaritan woman?" (John 4:9 NASB 1995). The conversation and the events that followed were nothing short of miraculous. By the end of their conversation, He had told her things that He hadn't told anyone else. He even told her that He was the Messiah that she had been waiting for. She became a believer and was so excited about what she had heard she forgot to take her waterpot when she left for home. Jesus' disciples returned right as He was finishing up his conversation with her. They were amazed that He was even talking to her, but they said nothing.

After she left, they went up to Him and urged Him to eat some of the food they had brought back. But He turned them down, saying, "**I have food to eat that you do not know about**" (John 4:32 NASB). He then said to them, "**My food is to do the will of Him who sent Me, and to finish His work. Do you not say, 'There are still four months and then comes the harvest'? Behold, I say to you, lift up your eyes and look at the fields, for they are already white for harvest!**" (vv. 34–35 NKJV).

Meanwhile, when the Samaritan woman arrived in her village, she told all of the men what had happened, and they believed her. They quickly traveled back to Sychar to hear Jesus in person. Then they, too, became believers that He was indeed the Messiah. They were so transformed, they urged Him to remain with them, and He spent the next two days personally teaching and discipling them. We can't imagine the number of people who became believers, followers, and disciples of Christ as a result of what happened in those three days.

What If Jesus Had Not Been in the Moment?

Now, let's make a slight change in the story. Jesus is sitting at the well. What would have happened if He had been focusing on the past? If He had been thinking, *I can't believe the argument that Peter and Philip had twenty minutes ago. I'm so tired of their bickering*? As He was reliving the past (focusing on just a few minutes earlier), the woman would have come to the well, filled her waterpot, and left. She would not have been born again. The men in the city would not have been born again. And Jesus would have continued His journey with no new believers or disciples. An entire city would have continued living in darkness without His light.

Say He was living just a few minutes in the future, thinking, *I can't wait till they get back; I am so hungry! I hope they bring Me some food that I like and not something that I don't like.* Once again, the woman would have come, filled up her waterpot, and left.

Or say He was living just eight hours into the future, thinking, *I can't wait until tonight. I'm going to spend all night in prayer, talking to My Father and listening to Him. Oh, what a blessed time we will have tonight when I can get away from everyone and spend time alone with Him.* Once again, the woman would have come and gone, and no eternal fruit would have been harvested by our Savior.

Fortunately, Jesus' mind and heart were not focused on the past or the future, but they were right in the moment with the Father and the Holy Spirit. When the woman arrived, He instantly drew her into His moment. Within minutes, the Holy Spirit birthed her—she was born again. And without even thinking about it, she became an unashamed witness and an evangelist for Jesus Christ. And dozens, maybe hundreds, and eventually maybe thousands of Samaritans became followers of Christ as a direct or indirect result of her witness. All of this took place because Jesus was in the moment when the woman arrived at the well.

> Jesus' mind and heart were not focused on the past or the future, but they were right in the moment with the Father and the Holy Spirit.

Thankfully, Jesus used this course of events to show and teach the disciples (and us) the critical nature of living in the moment. The disciples, like us, had a habit of living in the future. In their case, they were waiting for the next big event. Maybe the feeding of the five thousand. Maybe the healing of the blind or the raising of the dead. Maybe they were waiting for Jesus to declare Himself king and become the ruler of the ultimate kingdom. Sometimes they were even debating who would sit at His table in heaven (Mark 10:35–41). No matter what they were thinking at this moment, Jesus commanded them to open their eyes and see the fields they were standing in and harvest the fruit that was right in front of them—not in four months, or even two hours, but right now.

Jesus' commands are the same for us. He commands us to stop procrastinating ministry to those who cross our paths and to open our eyes and see the fields that are right in front of us. He's not commanding us to preach to everyone who is in our moment but rather to be His representative in the moment. If someone needs a hug, be His arms. If they need a word, be His mouth. If they need an ear, be His listening ear. If they need empathy, give them empathy. If they need wisdom or guidance, give them that, straight from the Savior's teachings. And if they need to hear the gospel, be His witness, in words and in deeds.

So how do we push the reset button to instantly take us out of the future or past and set our minds in the present moment?

Pushing the Reset Button

According to Harvard University, a study of 2,250 people showed that their minds were wandering and *not* in the present moment at least 46.9 percent of the time they were awake.[2] It's so easy to let our minds drift away from the moment. We don't even need an obvious distraction. It's our nature to focus on the past or the future. That's the bad news. It's bad because most of our negative thoughts and emotions enter our minds or hearts when we dwell in the past or the future. All stress, anxiety, worry, and fear enter our minds when we are thinking in the future. And most sadness, regret, anger, and resentment enter our minds and hearts when we are focused on the past. However, God's presence—and the joy, peace, and miracles that attend His presence—dwells *only* in the present. The good news is we can shift our focus into the present in an instant.

Red Flags That Instantly Tell Us We Are Not in the Moment

It's so easy and natural for our minds to wander out of the moment that we often need help to realize our thoughts have been hijacked by future-think or past-think. A number of red flags are instant signals that we are not dwelling in the present moment. Whenever you see them, let them alert you to immediately reset your focus into the present moment. As soon as you feel anxious, worried, fearful, or stressed, view those as red flags being waved at you to tell you that you are dwelling in the future. You have fallen into future-think. On the other hand, as soon as you feel sadness, regret, shame, bitterness, or resentment, view those as red flags being waved at you to alert you that you have drifted into the past, or past-think. You can easily activate a number of reset buttons to reset your focus. Any one of these will instantly bring you back into the present moment.

Red Flags That Signal You're in the Future	Red Flags That Signal You're in the Past
‣ Anxiety	‣ Sadness
‣ Fear	‣ Regret
‣ Stress	‣ Shame
‣ Dread	‣ Resentment
‣ Anticipation	‣ Nostalgia

Reset Buttons That Shift You into the Present

Let's start with the three reset buttons that Jesus revealed to His disciples right after His encounter with the woman at the well. He told them, "**Do you not say, 'There are yet four months, and *then* comes the harvest'? Behold**, I say to you, *lift up your eyes* and *look on the fields*, that they are white for *harvest*" (John 4:35 NASB 1995, emphasis added). Here, Jesus started the second sentence with the word *behold*. In the original language this word is extremely forceful. It is in the imperative tense, so it is a command. It is the same as Jesus saying, "Come into the moment right now, and really pay attention to what I'm about to tell you." And then He gave them the commands to (1) "**lift up your eyes**" and (2) "**look on the fields**." And because the fields are white, or ripe for harvest, His implied command is that they should (3) immediately begin harvesting. He went on to say that the reapers were already working in the fields, so get busy and start harvesting (v. 36). So here are the first three reset buttons that we can push to instantly bring us into the present moment.

Button #1: Lift Up Your Eyes

The first reset button is to "lift up your eyes." Whatever the eyes of your mind are looking at, whether back at past situations or forward at concerns of the future, you are to shift your focus immediately to the present moment. You can use little triggers like a quick blink, a nod of your head, taking an intentional deep breath, or even a pinch on your cheek. Regardless of how you do it, bring your physical eyes and your mental eyes into the present moment.

Button #2: Look On the Fields

The second reset button is to look around and see who is in that present moment with you. It might be a child or your spouse. It might be a coworker or a receptionist behind a desk. It might be an Uber driver or a server in a restaurant. If no one is physically present with you, it might be someone who comes to mind that you need to call or text. Whomever God directs your attention to, view them as a white field ready to harvest.

> Look around and see who is in that present moment with you.

Button #3: Begin the Harvest

The third reset button is to take action to begin harvesting. This doesn't mean you start preaching the gospel to the person; it means you become a representative of Jesus Christ to that person in that moment. They may need a smile, an appreciative look, a word of encouragement, a hug, or a listening ear. They may need you to pray for them or with them. They may want to tell you something they've just gone through. Or they may need to hear about our wonderful Savior and His amazing love for them. You don't have to force a situation. You simply need to be attentive to them. Most of the time, a smile, a nod, or even mere eye contact can convey that you appreciate and value them. If you're shy, don't panic. You don't even need to think about what you're going to say. You can ask them simple questions about themselves—as generic as "How are you this morning?" or "Any plans for the weekend?" or "Anything new with your kids?"

During the height of the Afghan war, I saw a uniformed serviceman walking toward me in the airport. I stopped him and thanked him for his service. He thanked me, and I asked, "Where are you headed?"

He replied, "I'm starting another tour in the Middle East."

I asked, "Could I just take a minute and pray for you?"

He said, "Yes, sir."

We bowed our heads, and I prayed a very short prayer for his safety and for his family and thanked God that He would be with this soldier throughout his tour. When I finished, he looked at me with tears in his eyes and said, "Sir, you have no idea how much this means to me. I'm leaving this airport and going to my deployment with a peace in my heart that I have never felt before." He reached out his hand, and after a strong handshake, we gave each other a hug. The whole encounter took less than three minutes, yet God had met us both in that present moment.

Bonus Button: Prayer

Another reset button that flips the switch to bring us out of the future or the past and into the present moment is prayer. The moment we see any of the red flags that signal we are not in the present moment, we can begin to pray—to have a simple conversation with God. We can pray about the issue we are dwelling on or about anything we are thinking about. In fact, God commanded us to do just that in Philippians 4:6–7. He told us, "Do not be anxious about anything, but in every situation, by prayer and petition, with thanksgiving, present your requests to God. And the peace of God, which transcends all understanding, will guard your hearts and your minds in Christ Jesus." It can be as quick as a couple of words or as long as we would like. Either way, it brings us instantly into the moment, and God is there.

The Essence of the Prayer Diamond

I like to compare prayer to a diamond. The top of a diamond is called the crown. The core or the biggest part of a diamond is called the pavilion. Finally, there are the many facets of the diamond. Although the crown and the facets highlight the diamond's beauty, the core or pavilion of the diamond gives the diamond its true essence—its depth, its clarity, its color, its strength, and its ultimate beauty and value. Like the diamond, prayer has a visible crown, and it has many facets, but most important is its core, its very essence. The true core or essence of prayer is honest, transparent communication with God in the present moment. Praying in this manner instantly empowers us to experience Joseph's principle of living in the present moment with God and others. This is what we see in Philippians 4:6–7.

Let's Break It Down

"Do not be anxious about anything, but in every situation, by prayer and petition, with thanksgiving, present your requests to God. And the peace of God, which transcends all understanding, will guard your hearts and your minds in Christ Jesus" (Phil. 4:6–7).

"Do not be anxious about anything."

This has a double meaning. First, it means don't be careful of what you share with God or ask of Him in prayer. Another way to say it would be, "Don't hold anything back." Paul is telling us to express to God exactly what's on our minds, no matter what it is, and say it without reservation. You don't have to sugarcoat anything you say, or anything you want, when you are talking to God. The second meaning is that we are to eliminate our worries and anxieties over future events by replacing them with the action of praying and petitioning God in the present.

> You don't have to sugarcoat anything you say, or anything you want, when you are talking to God.

"But in every situation, by prayer and petition, with thanksgiving."

Prayer is simply speaking words to God that express our thoughts and feelings. Petition ("supplication" in the King James Version) is praying for our actual desire(s) or request(s) that we want to ask of God. We're not holding anything back about any situation we're going through. We are telling God whatever we think and whatever we want in relation to that situation. And, at the same time, we are to thank God. If we are not able to sincerely thank Him for our situation, we are to thank Him for listening to us and loving us. No matter what situation we are going through, it must not overshadow or distract us from the fact that God has already proved His infinite love for us in sacrificing His Son for our sin and giving us the greatest gift of all time: eternal life (Rom. 5:8; John 3:16).

"Present your requests to God."

Simply stated, tell God what *you* want. Even if you know your desire is not what God wants, you are still commanded to tell Him your desire. There have been times when I have asked God for things that were totally self-centered and sometimes even things I knew were contrary to His will. But I still asked for them because they were what I truly wanted, whether He wanted them or not. I did not want His will; I wanted my will. As horrible as that may sound, that is what this passage commands us to do—honestly share our hearts and the desires that flow from it. However, the statement that follows in verse 7 explains and resolves everything.

"And the peace of God, which transcends all understanding, will guard your hearts and your minds in Christ Jesus."

Unlike so many other scriptures on prayer, this passage doesn't promise us the answers we are praying for. Instead, it promises us something infinitely better. It promises us "the peace of God," a peace so supernatural that it not only comes to us but actively guards our hearts and minds and keeps them safe in Jesus Himself. That peace may come the moment you obey God's command to honestly tell Him what you want, or it may come after a period of praying.

After I graduated from college, I was driving an ugly old beat-up

Studebaker station wagon. A friend of mine was selling his one-year-old Chevy Malibu Super Sport. I wanted that car more than I had ever wanted any material possession. Honestly, I wanted it whether it was God's will or not. In keeping with the commands here in Philippians 4:6–7, I prayed every day that God would give me the money to buy that car. Every day I told Him I wanted it whether it was His will or not. Finally, after a few days of telling God what I wanted, I heard His whispering. He asked me, "Do you want this car, even if it means you'll get hurt driving it? Do you want this car if it means you may hurt or kill someone else with it? Do you want this car even if it means your wife may die in it?"

With each question my heart became softer and my answers became stronger: "No, Lord, I *don't* want this car if it means *any* of these things!"

He then asked, "Do you want this car, or do you want *My* will?" Without hesitation, I then answered, "Lord, I want Your will," and I meant it. I didn't get the car, but I got something infinitely better. I received the priceless gift of God's peace. And with His peace, both my mind and my heart could and can easily remain and perform in the present moment.

Of course, the best example of this principle in action is found in the garden of Gethsemane. Jesus had never committed a single sin. He had never had a sinful thought or motive. Yet, as He considered what was coming the next day, He was certainly devastated and brokenhearted at the thought of actually taking on all of our sins. His dread was so great that He prayed and pleaded, "**My Father, if it is possible, let this cup pass from Me,**" but as quickly as He prayed those words, the peace of God came into His heart and He could sincerely pray, "**Yet not as I will, but as You will**" (Matt. 26:39 NASB). Two more times He prayed similar prayers, and two more times God's peace came into His heart and mind. By the third time, the peace of God had captured His heart, and nothing could prevent Him from completing His mission in the perfect way God had intended. The resulting peace that guarded His heart and mind was so powerful, it carried Him all the way through His impossible task.

Throughout my life I have found that whenever I pray honestly for what I truly want, God has ultimately delivered His peace to my heart, and then I could sincerely ask for His will rather than mine. Sometimes it's only taken minutes, and other times it's taken much longer. But the mere act of praying in accordance with Philippians 4:6–7 not only brings me peace; it always brings me into the present moment.

Since God first opened my eyes to living in the present moment, it has changed every single day. I have had the opportunity to show hundreds of people (mostly strangers) the kindness and love of Christ, just by paying attention to them and saying or doing things that show them they have true worth, to me and to God.

I recently traveled to New York City to visit my dear friend John, who was dying of cancer. John's wife, Carolee, had called me and told me that his condition was rapidly declining. I called Carolee as soon as I arrived in the city. She told me that one of John's favorite things was when people would bring him a milkshake. She said a little shop, Emack & Bolio's, made his favorite. She gave me the location, but I quickly forgot it and went to a different Emack & Bolio's location that was clear across town from their apartment. My daughter was driving me and dropped me off outside of the shop and drove around the block.

When I walked up to the door, it was locked, and my heart sank when I saw a sign that said it wouldn't open for another twenty minutes. I saw a woman in the shop who was hurriedly getting it ready to open. I smiled at her and raised my hands, trying to signal a plea of desperation. At first, she shook her head no, but I repeated my gesture. She then smiled and came to the door and unlocked it. I told her that my friend was dying and that he loved their milkshakes and asked if she could help me. She smiled again and invited me in. I didn't know which flavor my friend would prefer, so I asked her to make me two shakes, one vanilla and one chocolate.

For a moment, my mind drifted into the past as I thought about

John and our last visit four weeks earlier. Then my thoughts drifted into the future, and I started worrying about whether I would get to his apartment soon enough to have quality time with him. I wondered whether he would be cognizant or not. Then I realized I wasn't in the present moment. I quickly reset my focus and told the woman (Jojie) how grateful I was that she was helping me. I asked her where she was from, and she replied, "The Philippines." I told her that I had been to Manila numerous times and that I love the Filipino people. I then asked her if she owned the shop, and she told me that her sister and brother-in-law owned it. Her face saddened as she went on to tell me that her sister had very recently died of cancer, leaving behind her husband and children. I told her how sorry I was and asked if I could pray for her and her sister's family. She quickly said yes, and I put my arm around her and prayed.

When I finished, there were tears in her eyes, and she expressed her gratefulness. I told her that her kindness to open her shop twenty minutes early for a complete stranger was amazing to me. I said, "I do a lot of public speaking, and you are now one of the people I will talk about in the future."

She replied, "I'm not going to wait for the future. I'm going to talk about *you* tonight . . . as soon as I get home! I'm going to tell my whole family about you and that you prayed for us."

I tell this story to illustrate that had I not come into the moment, I would not have had the opportunity to experience God's amazing love for Jojie in that brief time we were together. I had a chance to show her that God knew her sorrow and loved her so much that He sent someone into her shop to express His love and care for her and her family. She was blessed, and I was blessed even more.

I promise you that if you will begin to follow Christ's commands to live in the moment, to see the fields and reap the harvest in front of you, you, too, will experience His wonderful love in the moment. You will have spontaneous opportunities to share His love nearly every remaining day of your life. If you get nothing else from this book, this principle and practice alone will miraculously transform every day, one moment at a time. You will experience the joy of seeing Him perform His wonderful and sometimes miraculous works in you and through you. God dwells only in the present moment, and so do His miracles.

> God dwells only in the present moment, and so do His miracles.

In light of everything you've just read, take one more look at the one thing that was worrying you at the beginning of this chapter. Think about the reset buttons you can push to shift your focus into the present moment whenever that worry enters your mind.

Now, take a look at the sorrows or regrets that tend to steal your mind from the present. Think about the reset buttons you can push to shift your focus into the present moment whenever those sorrows or regrets transport your mind and emotions into the past.

The more you practice using these reset buttons to retrieve your mind and bring it back into the present moment, the more natural it will become. As you see the incredible benefits and miracles that attend this practice, the more natural it will be for you to spend more and more of your waking hours in the present moment with God and those whom He brings into your path.

Joseph Principle #4: Living in the Moment with God and Others

Chapter 5

HEARING JESUS' WHISPERS—EVERY DAY

What I tell you in the dark, speak in
the daylight; what is whispered in
your ear, proclaim from the roofs.

Matthew 10:27

When we think of Joseph, likely the first things that come to mind are his dreams and interpretations of dreams. Yet, as we'll see in chapter 7, whenever the subject of interpretations came up, he was quick to point out that the interpretations were not his but rather God's. When Pharaoh asked Joseph to interpret his two dreams, Joseph emphatically stated, "I cannot do it . . . but God will give Pharaoh the answer he desires" (Gen. 41:16). Joseph knew that it was God who gave Pharaoh the dreams and God who would give Joseph the interpretations. How did God give those interpretations? He spoke them into Joseph's mind or spirit. Then, knowing that the interpretations had been whispered from God to him, Joseph confidently voiced those whispers to Pharaoh. We don't know how often Joseph received the whispers of God, but we know he did when it came to voicing interpretations. For all we know, he may also have heard the Lord's whisperings for the business decisions that made him remarkably successful. He may have heard the Lord's whisperings throughout his enslavement and imprisonments. Whether he heard them only when an interpretation of a dream was needed or heard them throughout his day, we don't know. But we *do* know he heard them.

Joseph Principle #5: Listening to the Whispers of God

On a trip to New York, I was invited to lunch by a Wall Street hedge fund manager. We were joined by his brilliant financial analyst and one of his major clients. All of us were committed followers of Jesus. They asked me where I was in my walk with Christ, and I told them I had spent the last ten years meditating on the teachings of Jesus contained in His nearly two thousand statements recorded in the Gospels. I told them there was no important question or issue they faced that Jesus had not addressed. I told them that in the past few years, whenever anyone brought me a sincere question, issue, or situation that they were dealing with, the Holy Spirit always whispered Jesus' words into my mind. And so far, His words had always revealed the answers and the solutions. Since I had been meditating on Jesus' words almost daily, the Holy Spirit was daily fulfilling the amazing promise that Jesus made in John 14:26. In that verse, speaking of the Holy Spirit, Jesus promised, **"He will teach you all things, and bring to your remembrance all that I said to you"** (NASB 1995).

I also told them that whenever anyone would ask me what Jesus said about something, without fail, the Holy Spirit would quickly bring a specific statement of Jesus into my mind that would answer their question.

I said, "People think I've memorized hundreds of Jesus' statements, but I haven't. The reason I can quote His statements that apply to their situations is because the Holy Spirit is performing His ministry of bringing Jesus' words and sayings into my mind."

The analyst decided to put this to the test and asked me a question that had been troubling her for some time. She said, "Okay, what would He say to me about this? As a committed Christian I have been saving myself for the man God would have me marry. I'm forty-seven, and He still hasn't brought that man into my life."

Instantly, the Holy Spirit whispered Jesus' words into my mind. I smiled at her and said, "Wow! God loves you *so* much! He reminded me that a sparrow doesn't fall to the ground apart from the will of your Father, and you are so much more valuable to Him than sparrows. He is protecting you, keeping you safe in His nest. Think of your friends who got married believing they would be so much happier, only to fall out of the nest onto the ground. So far, God has kept you in the nest for your own protection."

> A sparrow doesn't fall to the ground apart from the will of your Father, and you are so much more valuable to Him than sparrows.

As I said this, her eyes filled with tears. She then told us, "I'm crying because last year I asked the Lord to give me a verse that was just for me—a life verse that I could cling to for the rest of my life. The verse you just quoted is the exact verse He gave to me. And now He whispered that verse into your mind so you could remind me that this is God's answer for me!"

We were all astonished. There are approximately nineteen hundred statements of Jesus recorded in the Gospels, and the one He whispered to me in that moment was the very one He had given her for her life a year earlier. *That* is the ministry of the Holy Spirit promised in John 14:26, and it's available to all of us if we will consistently meditate on Jesus' words each week.

His Whispers Can Create Life-and-Death Miracles

Several years ago I was in a hotel room getting ready to speak to a group about my company and the science behind our new product. My cell phone rang, and when I answered, the words I heard were both shocking and devastating. I was told that my twenty-year-old son was coming home from Uruguay with a large, fast-growing tumor doctors had diagnosed as cancer. I was asked to use my influence to find the best surgeon I could to operate on Devin, as his life could be at stake. When we hung up, I fell onto the hotel bed, sobbing. I cried out to the Lord, reminding Him that my son was only twenty years old and I was fifty-nine—I told Him that *I* should be the one with cancer, not Devin.

At that moment, He whispered into my ear, "Open your book." I had spent two years working on a book where I organized the nineteen hundred statements of Jesus into 225 topics. The book, *The Greatest Words Ever Spoken*, wasn't coming out for four months, but my publisher, Random House, had made up four copies for a television interview I was to do the next day. I quickly ripped the wrapping off the pristine samples and opened the book. It opened to page 190 and the topic was *Anxiety, worry, and fear.* The very first red-lettered statement was "**It is I; don't be afraid**" (John 6:20). The next one was "**Don't let your hearts be troubled. Trust in God, and trust also in me**" (John 14:1 NLT).

As I read all the statements Jesus had made on this topic, I felt an amazing calmness come over me and a peace that was beyond my comprehension. But even though His reassurance and peace filled my heart,

I was still heartbroken over my son's condition and what he would soon be experiencing.

I then told the Lord there was no way I could go speak to the business group that night. He instantly whispered, "He who swears to his own hurt and does not change," from Psalm 15 (v. 4 NKJV). It's a verse I had read many times. It means when you've made a commitment and later discover that fulfilling that commitment is going to hurt you, you fulfill it anyway. He whispered, "You're to fulfill that commitment. Yesterday you told the people at two church services that you were going to speak at tonight's meeting, and they are showing up to listen. You must go!"

I said, "Lord, how will I even speak? All I can do right now is cry."

He said, "I will give you the words."

So, to the meeting I went. I gave my presentation, and then I told the audience what had happened. I asked them to pray in the week ahead that God would perform a miracle in my son's body. The pastor, whom I had known for only three days, came forward and said, "We're not going to wait; we're going to pray right now." He called up several of his leaders and they gathered around me, and he began to pray. He prayed, "Father, we know that You are the Great Physician, and nothing is too hard for You. And right now, in the name of Jesus Christ, I ask that You vaporize Devin's tumor . . . just make it disappear. And when the doctors open him up, let them tell our brother, 'I'm confused! I couldn't find the cancer! I don't understand this! I've never seen anything like this!' Then we'll know that You're the one who performed the miracle, and You alone will receive the glory."

When he finished praying, he looked down at me and said, "I just want you to know that God answered my prayer. Devin is fine. You have absolutely nothing to worry about." I was grateful for his prayer, but I really didn't believe his comment.

The next day, the head of urology at our university hospital agreed to see Devin and told me to bring him directly to the hospital when he arrived home in three days. When Devin landed on Friday, we didn't even take him to lunch—it was straight to the hospital, where he was examined by Dr. Blake Hamilton, head of resident urology at the University of Utah. After a brief physical, Dr. Hamilton called us into his office. He confirmed it was a cancerous tumor and told us he had scheduled surgery for Monday. Because of the size and location of the tumor, he told us there was a high likelihood it might have metastasized and spread, so they would scan his chest and brain once they confirmed the pathology on the tumor. If it had metastasized, Devin would have to undergo a long series of radiation and chemotherapy treatments.

Monday came, and the surgery began at half past noon. Two hours into the surgery the phone rang in the waiting room. The receptionist asked that Devin's parents come to the desk. She then looked at my wife and said, "Dr. Hamilton's still in surgery but wants to talk to you."

I had not told my wife about the pastor's prayer because I didn't believe it. She took the phone and moments later responded to the doctor's comments: "You're *confused*?" Then, after a few gasps and a few words, she hung up the phone.

I said to her, "Don't tell me—he said, 'I'm confused.'"

She was crying but replied, "Yes, he said he was confused."

I then said, "And he said, 'I couldn't find the cancer.'"

Surprised, she said, "Yes, he said he couldn't find the cancer. He sent out a frozen section to pathology, but it came back 'cancer free.'"

I said, "He said, 'I don't understand this.'"

"Yes," she said, "He said, 'I don't understand this, I don't understand this.'"

"And he said, 'I've never seen anything like this!'"

She caught her breath. "No, he didn't say that."

I then told her about the pastor's prayer one week earlier. She said, "He really prayed that?"

"Yes, out loud, in front of a hundred and fifty people." I then told her that the pastor had said that God had answered his prayer, that Devin was fine, and that I had absolutely nothing to worry about. I said, "Shannon, the tumor is gone, and the doctor said three out of four of the phrases, verbatim. The only phrase he didn't say was, 'I've never seen anything like this.'"

Needless to say, we were both amazed. Then, an hour later, Dr. Hamilton came into the waiting room, still in his scrubs, and sat down across from us. He threw his arms into the air, and the first words out of his mouth were, "I have *never* seen anything like this! All the damage from the cancer was there, but there was no cancer."

My son was cancer free! When I called the pastor the next day and told him what had happened, he quietly replied, "I know. I told you, 'God answered my prayer.'"

You see, not only had God performed the miracle that this humble pastor had prayed for, but the Holy Spirit had actually told him that his prayer had been answered. He believed with all of his heart that the tumor had been vaporized and that we would hear the surgeon say the four phrases he said. The Holy Spirit had revealed to the pastor "what is to come" (John 16:13 BSB).

> I will no longer let the limits of my faith cause me to deny *any* possible manifestation of the Spirit.

How often does this kind of manifestation of the Spirit take place today? How often will it take place in the future? I don't have the answer. But I do know that I will no longer let the limits of my faith cause me to deny *any* possible manifestation of the Spirit. I later found out that this particular pastor has the gift of faith, and this was not a unique experience in his lifetime of ministry.

Promptings of the Spirit and Whispers of Jesus

Most of the followers of Christ I know have experienced the minis-try of the Holy Spirit during their Christian experience. Most have had promptings from the Holy Spirit in various situations. Many have experienced the Holy Spirit bringing specific Bible verses or passages into their minds at opportune moments. Most of us have felt His con-viction and correction when we have failed to follow His promptings or disobeyed biblical teachings. Many have experienced the various gifts of the Spirit, and most have experienced the fruit of the Spirit. However, when I talk about hearing the *whispers* of Jesus, I'm talk-ing about something a little different. I'm talking about His command found in Matthew 10:27 and His promise found in John 14:26. In Matthew 10:27, Jesus said, "**What I tell you in the dark, speak in the daylight; what is whispered in your ear, proclaim from the roofs.**" Here, He is commanding His disciples to take what He says to them at night and proclaim it in the daytime and what is whispered in their ears to proclaim with strong conviction and confidence. When we add His teaching from John 14:26—that the Holy Spirit will remind us of everything Jesus said—we can deduce that if we meditate on the words and teachings of Jesus, the Holy Spirit will bring those very words and teachings to our minds right at the exact moment we need them. This is what I'm referring to when I talk about hearing the whispers Jesus referred to with His disciples.

My personal application of this fourth Joseph Principle was learning how to hear the whispers of Jesus. Fortunately, we have something much more practical and accessible than waiting for a dream or an interpre-tation of a dream. We have the most sure and rock-solid revelations of God's wisdom and His will ever recorded: the words of Jesus. Jesus said, "**Heaven and earth will pass away, but My words will never pass away**" (Matt. 24:35 BSB). Jesus made twenty-one promises about His words (His sayings and teachings) that He didn't make about any other words. His words have a role and power that are truly incomparable.

The Role and Power of Jesus' Words

"All Scripture is inspired by God and profitable for teaching, for reproof, for correction, for training in righteousness" (2 Tim. 3:16 NASB 1995). All scriptures were God-breathed and always given to us for specific purposes. Yet Jesus made very strong promises and claims concerning His words. The claims He made about His words He did not make about other words, sayings, or teachings found throughout the Bible. For example, Jesus said, **"The Spirit gives life; the flesh counts for nothing. The words I have spoken to you—they are full of the Spirit and life"** (John 6:63). Jesus' words not only bring revelation and inspiration; they are truly *full* of the Spirit and life. In my experience over the past fifteen years of daily meditating on Jesus' words, I have found that they deliver His Spirit and life into my spirit and life like no other words. They seem to go right through my mind, into my heart, and reach into the very depths of my soul and spirit. In times of discouragement, even despair, they go down deep and deliver a peace and confidence like nothing else.

Don't get me wrong—I've studied the Bible for more than fifty years, and God *always* uses whatever I read to accomplish whatever He wants to accomplish (Isa. 55:11). But Jesus' words are delivered with an authority and power beyond anything else I have ever experienced. After a large crowd finished listening to Jesus' Sermon on the Mount, Matthew wrote, "When Jesus had finished saying these things, the crowds were astonished at His teaching, because He taught as one who had authority, and not as their scribes" (Matt. 7:28–29 BSB). When the chief priests and Pharisees sent officers out to arrest Jesus and bring Him to them, the officers came back without Jesus. They were asked, "Why did you not bring Him?" The officers replied, "Never has a man spoken the way this man speaks" (John 7:46 NASB 1995). They went to arrest Him with their hearts as hard as stone, but as He spoke, their hearts melted, and they realized this man was not like any other. They didn't even try to arrest Him. Jesus later told another crowd, "**I have not spoken on My own, but the Father who sent Me has commanded Me what to say and how to say it**" (John 12:49 BSB).

"Listen to Him!"—God

Jesus took Peter, James, and John up onto a high mountain. There Jesus was transfigured, His face glowing as bright as the sun and His clothes becoming as white as light. Then Jesus was joined by the two most revered prophets in Israel's history, Moses and Elijah, and began talking with them. Peter then decided to put in his two cents and said, "Lord, it is good for us to be here. If you wish, I will put up three shelters—one for you, one for Moses and one for Elijah" (Matt. 17:4).

While Peter was still speaking, a bright cloud enveloped them and the angry voice of God said, "This is my Son, whom I love; with him I am well pleased. Listen to him!" (v. 5). How do we know it was the *angry* voice of God? Because the next verse tells us that Peter, James, and John "fell facedown to the ground, terrified" (v. 6). At Jesus' baptism, the witnesses heard God lovingly say, "This is My beloved Son, in whom I am well pleased" (Matt. 3:17 NKJV), and no one was terrified. At the transfiguration, God was indicating Peter was horribly wrong in saying he would erect three shelters that would serve as monuments to Jesus and the two prophets. God was announcing loud and clear that since Jesus' arrival on earth, He and His words superseded all the prophets and all of their words. Jesus was truly God's ultimate Word. While Moses and the other prophets were mere men, God was making the point that Jesus was His beloved Son. In fact, Jesus would soon be going to the cross to save Moses, Elijah, and all of the other prophets from their sins. I would imagine God was saying, "How dare you compare these or any other man to My Son! Listen to Him and do what He says!"

Inspired by the same God who spoke at the transfiguration, the writer of Hebrews wrote, "In the past God spoke to our ancestors through the prophets at many times and in various ways, but in these last days he has spoken to us by his Son, whom he appointed heir of all things, and through whom also he made the universe. The Son is the radiance of God's glory and the exact representation of his being, sustaining all things by his powerful word" (1:1–3).

And finally, at the Last Supper, Jesus told His disciples, "**The words I say to you I do not speak on my own authority. Rather, it is the Father, living in me, who is doing his work**" (John 14:10).

Are you beginning to see the basis of why I contend that Jesus' words, full of His Spirit and life, can transform the human heart like no

> Jesus' words, full of His Spirit and life, can transform the human heart like no other words ever spoken.

other words ever spoken? This is why I also say that to consistently hear His whispers, we must thoughtfully and prayerfully read His words every day. I hope you will begin to feast on His words and His life as recorded in the Gospels. Nothing you will ever do in your lifetime will affect your life and the lives of those you influence more than this simple practice. I don't say this according to my wisdom but according to the promises of Jesus in His statements about His sayings and teachings. Below is a list of the twenty-one amazing promises Jesus made about His words.

21 Promises Jesus Made About His Words and His Words Only

1. They will provide an ongoing infusion of His Spirit and life into your spirit and life (John 6:63).
2. They provide the way for you to become Jesus' true disciple (John 8:31).
3. They provide the way for you to intimately know the truth (John 8:32).
4. You will be liberated from enslavement to sin (John 8:32–38).
5. You will gain intimacy with Jesus and the Father (John 14:21–23).
6. You will be loved in a special way by the Son and the Father (John 14:21–23).
7. Jesus will reveal Himself, His heart, and His mind to you (John 14:21–23).
8. The Father and the Son will come to you (John 14:23).
9. The Father and the Son will make Their continual dwelling place with you (John 14:23).
10. You will be cleansed from your sin (John 15:3).
11. Your prayer requests will be answered (John 15:7).
12. You will bear much eternal fruit (John 15:8).
13. You will glorify the Father (John 15:8).
14. You will remain in the center of Jesus' love (John 15:10).
15. Jesus' joy will be in you (John 15:11).
16. Your joy will be full (John 15:11).
17. The "house" of your life will never be destroyed (Matt. 7:24–25).
18. Your life will be built on the perfect foundation (Matt. 7:24–25).
19. You will be intimately known by Jesus (Matt. 7:21–25).
20. You will have assurance of your eternal life (Matt. 7:24–25).
21. Your life and faith will never be shaken (Matt. 7:24–25).

Receiving Jesus' twenty-one promises about His words has only one condition: begin to abide in His words. Abiding in His words means regularly and thoughtfully reading them in the Gospels and letting His words provide the instructions and guidelines for your attitudes and behaviors. His promises and commands and teachings provide the step-by-step path for following Him. And with each step you take, your faith will grow and the miracles that will accompany your walk with Him will abound.

Joseph Principle #5: Listening to the Whispers of God

Chapter 6

GOD'S LOVE LANGUAGE

We love Him because He first loved us.

1 John 4:19 NKJV

W hen we think of Joseph, we instantly associate certain images with him. We think of his robe of many colors that Jacob gave to him. We think of his dreams of grandeur that made his brothers envious. We think of his being sold into slavery or being tempted by Potiphar's wife. Of course, we think of the interpretations of dreams. We think of his revelation of the sovereignty of God or his forgiveness of his brothers. While all of these descriptors are true, they are not what he was most recognized for by those in authority over him.

From the time he was sold into slavery, Joseph had only three authorities that he was accountable to: Potiphar, the prison warden, and Pharaoh. All three of these men were amazed by one of Joseph's traits: his success. His success was so amazing that each of the three turned over all of their managing and governing authority to him, because everything he managed was successful beyond their imaginations. All three correctly deduced that the only way he could be so successful was that God was with him (Gen. 39:3, 21; 41:37–44).

Joseph had a truly intimate relationship with God, and everything he did that created his success flowed out of that relationship. They knew it, and Joseph knew that everything he valued in life was his because of his intimate relationship with God—*everything*. He was incredibly confident, but his confidence was not in himself. He had no self-confidence. All of his confidence, 100 percent of his confidence, was in God and His loving sovereignty. And of course, that confidence flowed out of his intimate relationship with God. His incredible faith, love, and forgiveness in spite of his terrible adversities flowed out of this intimacy.

Hopefully, you are seeing this glorious picture. If you are seeing it, like me, you may be thinking, *Oh, how I wish I could have that kind of relationship with God, one that would create in me what it created in Joseph—a supernatural level of trust and faith. A level of love for God and others that could enable me to forgive the unforgivable. A level of faith that would enable me to please and glorify God and work miracles all around me.* Well, here's the best news you'll hear today: you *can* have this level of intimacy with God.

> Our goal must be gaining the level of intimacy with God that Joseph had.

Perhaps now you are recoiling a bit at that statement, thinking, *No way! Not me. I don't have anything near that kind of faith.* You're right, you don't have that kind of faith. But if that's what you're saying, you're missing the point. That kind of faith is a blessing that flows out of an intimate relationship with God. Our goal must not be gaining Joseph's faith, wisdom, or spiritual gifts. Our goal must be gaining the level of intimacy with God that Joseph had. That must be our focus and our goal.

You may be wondering, *How on earth could I ever have that kind of intimacy with God?* The absolute truth is you can have that same level of intimacy with the Father—and an even greater level of intimacy, because you have three resources that Joseph didn't have. First, if you've been born again, the Holy Spirit has taken up residency in your spirit, so you have access to all of the fruits of the Spirit. Second, thanks to the Gospels, you have a glorious record of the life of Jesus that Joseph did not have, a life that perfectly reveals the Father. And finally, you have access to the recorded words of the Messiah that Joseph never had. Those words provide the very means by which you can move into a level of intimacy with God that is even greater than Joseph experienced. That is what Jesus proclaimed. He not only revealed that we could have that kind of relationship but also gave us the precise instructions we could follow to experience that kind of intimate relationship.

Intimacy with the Father and the Son

When I talk about knowing God intimately, I am not talking about whether you are religious, a Christian, or even a diligent Bible student. Sadly, most of us define or assess our relationship with God by the level of Bible knowledge we have or by how much time we spend studying Scripture. As wonderful as these attributes may be, in themselves they do not create one-on-one intimacy with Jesus and God the Father. In fact, Jesus criticized the most religious, most knowledgeable Bible students of His day. He told them, **"You study the Scriptures diligently because you think that in them you have eternal life. These are the very Scriptures that testify about me, yet you refuse to come to me to have life"** (John 5:39–40).

Our relationship with God and His Son cannot be measured by our knowledge of the Bible or by our religious activities. Here, Jesus is telling us that our relationship with God and our eternal destiny that flows from Him can be experienced only by coming to Jesus for that life, both here on earth and in our eternal life. Jesus reinforced this teaching when He said in His intercessory prayer, "**Now this is eternal life: that they know you, the only true God, and Jesus Christ, whom you have sent**" (John 17:3). The Greek word used in this passage means "intimately know." So eternal life is experienced by *intimately* knowing the Father and the Son. Jesus tells us how to experience this intimacy when He reveals God's love language.

In his book *The Five Love Languages*, Gary Chapman teaches that all of us have a love language. In other words, we want to be loved in one of five ways. He calls the way we want to be loved our love language. The five love languages Gary identifies are (1) words of affirmation, (2) physical touch, (3) receiving gifts, (4) quality time, and (5) acts of service. My love language is words of affirmation. So, if one person gives me a physical gift, and another person gives me sincere words of affirmation, I will feel more loved by receiving the words than I will by receiving the physical gift. Even though the person who gives me the physical gift may truly love me more than the one who gives me the affirming words, I will *feel* more loved by the one who loves me using my love language. At the same time, if I love someone with words of affirmation and their love language is physical gifts, even though I'm sincerely loving them, they may not feel my love because I'm not using *their* love language. I'm loving them the way that's easiest for me but much less powerful for them.

For most of my life, I was a diligent Bible student and Bible teacher. But then, in 2005, I discovered the unique role and power of Jesus' spoken words. In His words, Jesus revealed many of the great mysteries of life. One such mystery was how we can have true, moment-by-moment intimacy with Him and the Father. And to my surprise, Jesus' revelation was much different than I had imagined. In fact, in Gary Chapman's vernacular, Jesus revealed His and God the Father's love language. He promised that He and the Father would enter into a uniquely intimate relationship with anyone who would love the Father and Himself in this very specific way.

To the man, woman, boy, or girl who loves God in this way (using His love language), Jesus promised, "**My Father will love them. And I will love them and reveal myself to each of them**" (John 14:21 NLT). Moments later He added, "**My Father will love them, and we will come and make our home with each of them**" (v. 23 NLT). To those who will love Jesus and the Father in this particular way, Jesus promised that He and the Father will love them in a special, intimate way to the point that Jesus will personally reveal Himself to them and that He and the Father will make Their continual dwelling place with them. *That* is true intimacy with God!

Hopefully, you're asking the question, "What is this love language that Jesus promises that He and the Father will respond to in such a miraculous and intimate way?" As it turns out, Jesus revealed that His and the Father's love language is obeying the teachings and commands of Jesus (John 14:21). Literally, hearing what Jesus says and *doing* it. Here are Jesus' amazing promises in their context:

> "**Whoever has my commands and keeps them is the one who loves me. The one who loves me will be loved by my Father, and I too will love them and show myself to them.**"
>
> **Then Judas (not Judas Iscariot) said, "But, Lord, why do you intend to show yourself to us and not to the world?"**
>
> **Jesus replied, "Anyone who loves me will obey my teaching. My Father will love them, and we will come to them and make our home with them. Anyone who does not love me will not obey my teaching. These words you hear are not my own; they belong to the Father who sent me."** (John 14:21–24)

So let's break this one down.

1. Jesus' and the Father's love language is not our normal emotion-based love but rather is a very pragmatic love. It is literally hearing what Jesus said and then doing what He said. It is hearing His instructions and teachings and then acting in faith, obeying those instructions and teachings by doing them. Not complicated at all.

2. When we are in various situations and question what choice we should make, we should ask, "What did Jesus say?" According to another one of Jesus' promises, the Holy Spirit will remind us of what He said; we then express our love for the Father and the Son by doing what He said (John 14:26). By the way, Jesus never gives us an instruction without supplying us with the grace and power to do what He said (1 Cor. 10:13). And Jesus' commands (unlike the commands of the law) do not burden or overwhelm us (1 John 5:3). In fact, as you will discover, Jesus' commands are empowering. They are like rocket fuel in the engine of our soul. They enable us to "blast off" with His awesome power and soar above any of the problems that distract or obstruct us.

3. As we show our love for Him by hearing and doing what He says, He and the Father will love us in a very special way. And Jesus will show us that special love by revealing His heart and desires and His wisdom.

4. Jesus and the Father will come to us and make Their continual dwelling place with us. How amazing that the God of the universe and His Son would come to you and me and dwell with us wherever we reside. Whether we are in a house, an apartment, a tent, a boat, or in a sleeping bag in the desert, the Father and the Son will be present with us as we love Them the way They want to be loved.

What Does This Mean to Us in Our Struggles with Adversity, Heartaches, and Loneliness?

This is the biggest game changer of all time. Imagine yourself in the middle of the greatest trial and heartache of your life. Now imagine that Jesus suddenly appears in your room. Would your focus instantly shift from everything else you were thinking about and everything else you were feeling toward Him? Would you run to His side to hear His voice and receive His comfort, encouragement, and directions? Would your loneliness be instantly dispelled?

Of course the answer is yes to all of the above. You may not physically see Jesus or the Father, but when you begin to put more focus on hearing and doing what Jesus says, the Father and Son will come to you; They will make Their continual dwelling place with you, and through the Holy Spirit you will experience Their moment-by-moment presence, peace, and love.

You will also hear the Holy Spirit bringing Jesus' words into your mind, and you will hear the whispers of the Lord in your mind's ear. For example, you may hear Jesus whisper, "Come unto Me, my dear child, and let Me carry the heavy load of your weary and broken heart. I am humble and gentle of heart, and you can safely put your trust in Me" (Matt. 11:28–29). Jesus said, **"My sheep hear My voice, and I know them [intimately], and they follow Me"** (John 10:27 NASB 1995). This is how you position yourself next to the Good Shepherd so you can hear His voice and get to know Him more and more intimately each day. In fact, according to Jesus, this kind of intimacy is the very essence of eternal life. He said in His intercessory

> When you begin to put more focus on hearing and doing what Jesus says, the Father and the Son will come to you.

prayer the night of His arrest, "**This is eternal life, that they may [inti-mately] know You, the only true God, and Jesus Christ whom You have sent**" (John 17:3 NASB 1995).

Your reaction may be, "I know Jesus, and I know what He said, and it doesn't make that much of a difference." Friend, if it doesn't make that much of a difference, then you really don't know what Jesus said. And if you don't know what He said, you don't know Him the way He wants to be known. Remember, His condition for this level of intimacy is that you begin to listen to His commands and teachings and follow Him by doing them. As obvious as this may seem, and as fundamental as it may be to following Christ, it has not been the widespread message of most evangelicals. I've been with many pastors and even some of the world's most respected Christian leaders who have been shocked when I've asked them if they knew that Jesus gave over 150 loving and empowering commands to His followers.[1] Some have struggled to even name ten; they've also been shocked when I've mentioned that Jesus gave over eighty conditional promises to His followers.[2]

During my lifetime, I've found a lot of Christians who were good Bible students, but only a handful who knew the commands, promises, and teachings of Christ. Yet these are the very words Jesus and the Father have told us to focus on in our daily lives. They provide the very foundation and basis for walking by faith. They not only bring us into intimacy with God but also grow and strengthen our faith. They bring tremendous love, compassion, truth, and power to us and to our ministry. And they are the very means the Holy Spirit uses to make us disciples and to empower us to make disciples of others (Matt. 28:19–20).

Sound overwhelming? I promise you, it's not. Addition and subtraction were overwhelming when you were first starting to learn arithmetic. But once you took on the normal everyday practice of adding and subtracting, they weren't overwhelming at all. The same is true with the commands, promises, and teachings of Christ.

What Specifically Does Jesus Say to Those Who Are Going Through Trials and Dealing with Heartbreak or Loneliness?

In the areas of adversity, heartbreak, and loneliness, Jesus said a great deal. He gave us everything we need—comfort, companionship, guidance, and solutions. For example, let's look at His commands and promises found in Matthew 11:28–30: "**Come to me, all you who are weary and burdened, and I will give you rest. Take my yoke upon you and learn from me, for I am gentle and humble in heart, and you will find rest for your souls. For my yoke is easy and my burden is light.**" Let's break it down:

1. If we are weary (worn out, stressed, anxious, or fearful) and burdened (grieving, overwhelmed, crushed), then He commands us: "**Come to me.**" Our nature is to go to others first, and if we go to Jesus at all, we go to Him last. Yes, we may pray and ask His help and guidance, but here He's commanding much more. He says we must come to Him with our hearts, our minds, our voices, and most important, our ears—to hear His words of comfort, love, truth, and guidance.

2. If we obey His command to come to Him, He promises that He will give us rest (total relief) from all of the burdens we've been carrying. The Greek word used here for "rest" means "total relief"—that is, the stopping of all labor and receiving rest and physical refreshment. The labor in this case is all of the mental, emotional, and physical stress and effort we are expending in our effort to carry our burdens rather than giving them to Him.

3. He commands us to take on His yoke. The yoke Jesus is talking about here is not the type of yoke that harnesses oxen together. Here, Jesus is talking about a rabbinical yoke. A rabbinical yoke refers to a rabbi's unique interpretations of the law and

their particular teachings on how to apply the law to one's life. While the rabbinical yokes of most rabbis added tremendous man-made burdens to the spiritual shoulders of their disciples, Jesus was telling His disciples (and us) that His yoke is just the opposite. His yoke lightens our load rather than increasing our burden.

4. He commands us to "**learn from me.**" Where do you draw your knowledge from to guide your attitudes and behaviors? TV and movies? The internet? Friends and relatives? Educators, therapists, books, or magazines? Pastors, counselors, or other religious authorities? No matter how good any of these may be, Jesus was saying that first and foremost, you should learn from Him. Learn from His teachings in the Gospels, and learn from the shining examples of His life, His attitudes, and His behavior. Then you will have His ultimate truths by which you can measure all of the purported truths and values of others. You can view all of life through the lens of His teachings and life.

5. He promises to lead, guide, and teach you gently, from a heart of humility. Jesus is not a policeman, a judge, or a religious dictator. He is a humble, loving, and gentle shepherd who adores His Father and loves His sheep. And when He teaches us through His words or the example of His life, He will do so with tenderness and humility.

6. He promises that our souls (the very depth of our beings—who we really are) will find total relief and rest from our burdens. When we harness ourselves to Jesus and learn from Him, His words will infuse His Spirit and life into our spirit and life, and the incomprehensible peace and joy that we experience won't just be a mental or emotional high but will reach into the depths of our souls and gradually transform the very core of who we are.

7. His yoke is easy, and His burden is light. Here Jesus promised that unlike the yokes of other religious teachers that add to one's burdens, His yoke is truly easy and the burden it creates is truly light. He's beckoning you to trade your heavy burden for His lighter one. He tells us all of this so that we will not even hesitate to leave our burdens with Him. As we do, we will enter into His promised rest and be refreshed.

We see Him do all of this at the Last Supper (John 13–16). He went out of His way to ease the stress and paralyzing angst of His disciples. Jesus was about to be arrested, ruthlessly beaten, scourged, and crucified. Even worse, He was about to take on the sewage of our sins and be separated from the Father for the first time in eternity. All of this was ahead of Him, but His focus remained on serving, relieving, instructing, and encouraging His disciples so they wouldn't be taken by surprise and would ultimately experience His overwhelming joy. He said, "**These things have I spoken to you, that my joy may be in you, and that your joy may be full**" (John 15:11 ESV). He was about to be burdened with the sins of all mankind, yet He still had room to take on the full weight of their burdens. My friend, He wants to do the same thing for you and me.

No Trial, No Matter How Terrible, Has Happened to You or Your Loved Ones Outside of God's Watchful Eye and Sovereign Love

When Joseph proclaimed to his brothers, "You meant it for evil, but God meant it for good" (Gen. 50:20), he revealed the glorious truth of God's sovereignty, even to the point of His overcoming the evil acts of men to bring about His glorious will—even to the point of saving whole nations. In business, we call that "the view from thirty thousand feet" or the macro view. But Jesus doesn't leave it there. He gives us the view at ground level—the micro view. He shows us that there is absolutely no negative or adverse event in our lives that happens to us without first passing through God's loving will (Matt. 10:29–31).

When we experience heartbreaking or even life-shattering events, it's so easy to think, *God doesn't care* or *How could God let this happen? I thought He loved us.* But Jesus tells you and me that God loves us so much He cares about even the tiniest detail of our lives, even to the point of knowing the number of hairs on our head. And if a single sparrow can't fall to the ground apart from His love, neither can anything happen to us apart from His love. Consequently, we can fully trust that He is with us in every circumstance—every moment of our day and night. As I mentioned at the beginning of this book, when adversity comes our way, it will either interrupt and obstruct our fellowship with God or it will become a springboard to a more intimate relationship with Him. When we embrace a faulty assessment that He either doesn't care or is not present, the adversity becomes a roadblock to our fellowship with God. To get past that roadblock, we must replace our faulty assessment or appraisal with an accurate one.

> There is absolutely no negative event in our lives that happens to us without first passing through God's loving will.

Our Perspective and Judgments Are Limited by What We Can See—God's Judgments Are Not

The reason we can make such faulty appraisals of God and His love for us when adversity strikes is because we see adversity only in relation to our mortal life here on earth. We make our judgments by measuring all events and experiences in relation to our time on earth—a time James described as nothing more than a temporary mist that appears in the morning, then quickly vanishes with the rising sun (James 4:14). God, on the other hand, sees everything in the light of eternity and His glorious will, which cannot be contained within our tiny box of time. God's love and mercy, His righteousness, justice, and judgment, do not have to be fully disclosed, executed, or experienced within the confines of time. He has all eternity to express His love and execute His justice.

As a believer in Christ who has been born again, you are an eternal spirit housed in a temporary body. Jesus wants us to begin to see our lives and everything in them from God's eternal point of view—and act accordingly by hearing and doing what Jesus says. The apostle Paul revealed that the adversity we experience here on earth can spread God's grace to more and more people, and the affliction itself produces for us an incomparable degree of eternal glory that dwarfs any pain we experience here on earth. He then told us that anything we see or feel is only temporary, but the things we don't see or feel are eternal (2 Cor. 4:16–18).

So What Am I Supposed to Do?

Jesus didn't just give us principles. He detailed specific actions we can take. Here are just a few of the steps He told us to take each day.

- **Take control of our hearts**. He told us to do this by actively believing in Him and the Father. He was not referring to a mere mental acceptance but rather a belief that is expressed by doing what Jesus says (John 14:1).

- **Hear and do**. He told us to build our lives on the rock of hearing His words and obeying them instead of on the sand of hearing His words and not doing them (Matt. 7:24–27). He promised that if you will begin to hear His teachings and do them, no matter how badly you are assaulted by the storms of life, you will have everything you need from Him to endure and overcome all your adversity.

- **Remind and rejoice**. Every day, throughout each day, remind yourself of what the Father and the Son have done for you so you can have eternal life, and rejoice that your name has been permanently recorded in heaven (John 3:16; Luke 10:20). Start today.

- **Meditate on Jesus' words**. Every day, thoughtfully read Jesus' teachings found in the gospels of Matthew, Mark, Luke, and John. Or read His teachings by topics in *The Greatest Words Ever Spoken: Everything Jesus Said About You, Your Life, and Everything Else*.[3] Thoughtfully and prayerfully reading His words sets your mind and heart in a place where the Holy Spirit can perform His ministry of teaching you all things and bringing to your memory whatever Jesus said (John 8:31–32, 14:26).

- **Pray in secret**. Jesus said that if you will go off by yourself and take your requests to the Father in secret, He will reward you (Matt. 6:6). Of course, there is nothing wrong with praying in a group together with others. However, going off by yourself where it is just you and God creates a setting where two hearts can come into unity and where even the slightest whispers can be heard and felt. The reward that Jesus promised you'll receive from the Father is a greater unity with Him and a quietness in which you can hear the whispers of the Father and Son conveyed by the Holy Spirit. And don't be surprised if you gain a much greater desire for His will to be done in your life and in the situations you are dealing with. Your reward will include the revelation of His will, the remembrance of

Jesus' words, and the empowerment to go forward into your day with more assurance, confidence, courage, and love.

- **Listen for His whispers.** In Matthew 10:27, Jesus told us, **"What I tell you in the dark, speak in the daylight; what is whispered in your ear, proclaim from the roofs."** I've now been reading and meditating on Jesus' words for about fifteen years. Almost from the beginning of this practice, I have experienced the Holy Spirit performing His ministry of bringing Jesus' words to my memory whenever I need them. Oftentimes, when I'm facing a question or a choice, the Holy Spirit will perform His ministry, whispering into my mind the words of Jesus that are applicable to that specific question or choice. Sadly, there have been times when I've chosen to ignore His whispers and stubbornly do what I wanted to do rather than what He wanted me to do. And in doing so, I've not only harmed myself but also deeply hurt others.

Do the Father and Jesus *Really* Want Intimacy with Us?

As hard as it may be to believe, the answer to this question is a resounding yes. And that yes comes right from the voices of the Father and the Son Themselves. Jeremiah wrote,

Thus says the LORD.

> "Let not the wise man glory in his wisdom,
> Let not the mighty man glory in his might,
> Nor let the rich man glory in his riches;
> But let him who glories glory in this,
> That he understands and [intimately] knows Me,

That I am the LORD, exercising lovingkindness, judgment,

and righteousness in the earth.

For in these I delight," says the LORD. (Jer. 9:23–24 NKJV)

God said that the great joy and purpose of our life—our glory—should flow out of our intimacy with Him. The word translated as "knows" in this passage is the Hebrew word for "intimately knowing." If intimacy with God isn't your great joy and glory, don't fret. As your daily focus becomes hearing and doing what Jesus says, your intimacy with God will become more and more your glory. And as we saw earlier, Jesus went even further in His prayer in John 17:3. He revealed that intimately knowing Him and the Father was the very essence of eternal life. Your eternal life doesn't begin when you die. It begins while you are alive on earth. And it is experienced moment-by-moment as you live in intimacy with the Father and the Son.

If God says that intimacy with Him is to be our glory and Jesus equates eternal life with intimately knowing Him and the Father, then of course They want intimacy with us. Knowing that Jesus defined eternal life as intimately knowing Him and the Father, take a fresh look at John 3:16: **"For God so loved the world that he gave his one and only Son, that whoever believes in him shall not perish but have eternal life."** When you believe in Christ to the point of hearing and doing what He says, you will have eternal life—intimacy with the only true God and Jesus Christ whom He sent.

Please know that I am not saying we gain eternal life by doing what Jesus tells us to do. Eternal life is a gift that God gives to all who believe in His Son. We do what Jesus said because we've received His gift. Doing what Jesus said is God's love language, and it's our way of loving Him back in the way *He* wants to be loved!

Review

Read John 14:21–24 and then, in your own words, write out what Jesus is saying to you.

_____

_____

_____

_____

Chapter 7

MIRACLES EVERY DAY

God Makes the Deposits—
You Write the Checks!

> Most assuredly, I say to you, he who
> believes in Me, the works that I do he will
> do also; and greater works than these he
> will do, because I go to My Father.
> *John 14:12 NKJV*

A few months ago a dear friend of our family called us from another state. My wife, Shannon, answered the phone and heard Tammy sobbing on the other end. Tammy told Shannon that her best friend's eighteen-year-old son had just been killed in a head-on crash with a semi-truck. We turned on the ten o'clock news, and sure enough, one of the first stories was about this crash. We jumped on the internet and found the story on a TV news site. The boy had been killed instantly.

In the past, I had a ministry with parents who had lost children through car accidents, cancer, suicides, and even murder. It's not a ministry I ever sought out, but God just put me in the right places at the right times. As I watched the TV report, God put a yearning in my heart to minister to the young man's parents, and for some reason my yearning mainly revolved around wanting to talk with his father. But I knew that now was not the right time. I silently prayed, *Lord, if this yearning is from You, You'll have to create the opportunity for me to meet the parents.*

About a month later, Tammy and her family came to Utah for a ski vacation. My wife and I drove to see them at the condo they were renting. Amazingly, the mother and father of the boy who was killed were staying with them. My wife and I had no idea they would be there.

The ladies decided to go into town for a while, leaving me and the father alone in the condo. God had answered my prayer; He'd put me in the same town, in the same condo, and on the same sofa with the man He had given me a burden for.

As we began to talk, the father told me of his family's relationship with Tammy's family. And then he said, "I lost my son a few weeks ago in a car accident." I told him how sorry I was, and then we were both quiet for a moment. He then said, "You know, when you lose a child, all your friends and relatives focus on the mom. No one really thinks about what the dad is going through—you're kind of left alone."

When he said that, I thought, *Not this time!* God had brought us together through no planning of our own, and though he didn't know it, this man had a new friend for life.

He told me he was reexamining everything about his religion, and he didn't know how he felt about it. I told him that I understood. I said, "I've known other families who have lost children, and I have seen other fathers go through the same reassessment of their religions." I said, "I don't know if you've realized it yet, but religion really falls short. It doesn't get down to the deepest levels of your soul where you're hurting so badly."

He instantly responded, "You're right! It doesn't even *touch* the pain."

I said, "On the other hand, Jesus does deal with every aspect of our hearts and souls, and He can touch the pain and soothe the anguish. But He doesn't do it mystically or magically. He offers us His words and solutions. If we listen and do what He tells us, then miracles happen. As horrible as this season is for you, it can be a time for you to move into a level of intimacy with Jesus that will be deeper and more fulfilling than you have ever known."

He said, "I'm not walking away from Jesus. I *want* to get to know Him better."

I told him that I left atheism when I became fully persuaded that Jesus was the person He said He was. I told him, "I've never been religious, but for the past fifty-six years, Jesus has not only been my Lord and Savior, He's been my best friend—and a miracle-working friend at that!"

That was the beginning of my friendship with David—a friendship that I expect will last for the rest of my life. We've been together since that night, and God has really blessed our time together.

I share this story as an example of the hundreds of miracles I've experienced in my life since becoming a follower of Christ. But to be honest, those are the miracles I've *seen*. In my fifty-plus years as a believer, there are likely *thousands* of miracles that have happened to me and around me that I haven't seen. For example, I was speaking at a meeting in Toronto. After the meeting, a fifty-five-year-old man asked me if he could take a couple of minutes to tell me his story. He had been in a terrible car accident that left him completely incapacitated. His wife left him, and he lost his job and his career as a government auditor. He moved into the basement of his parents' home. His recuperation was very slow, and after a year, he was very depressed.

One afternoon his parents told him they were going out for lunch. He said to me, "I had been thinking about suicide for a long time, and I decided that while they were out would be the perfect time." He wrote a note to his folks and brought a stool down to the basement. He hung a rope from the rafter. His television was on at the time.

As he was positioning the stool, the Christian TV show *100 Huntley Street* came on, and he heard the host introducing me. He left the stool for a moment, because something I said piqued his curiosity. He sat down on the sofa and listened more intently, and he heard me talking about Jesus as if He were alive today. He said to me, "You were talking about Him like He was your best friend."

I quickly replied, "He is!"

The man told me he kept listening to the show, and at the end when I prayed, he prayed with me and asked Jesus to forgive his sins and to come into his heart and be his Lord and Savior. He said, "After I stopped crying, I took the stool back upstairs, tore up the note, and here I am."

This is what I mean when I say there may have been thousands of miracles happening around me that I've never seen. I wouldn't have learned about this one had this man not come to the meeting to hear me speak. (Also, anybody who has ever been with me in a car knows that it's a miracle I'm still alive. According to a university physician who tested me, I'm the most ADD person he's ever tested—out of thousands. Who knows how many car accidents God has miraculously prevented from happening to me?)

Would You Like to See Miracles Become an Everyday Experience in Your Life?

Would you like to see more miracles in your life? (That's probably the dumbest question you've ever been asked.) Joseph experienced miracles. We don't know how many or how often, but we know God was with him (Gen. 39.2), and when God is with anyone the way He was with Joseph, miracles will surround them.

Did you know that Joseph *never* interpreted anyone's dreams? Two members of Pharaoh's household staff were thrown into the same prison as Joseph. They both had dreams on the same night. The next morning, Joseph asked why they were looking so sad, and they replied, "We both had dreams . . . but there is no one to interpret them." Joseph said to them, "Do not interpretations belong to God?" (Gen. 40:6–8). In other words, Joseph didn't have the gift of interpretation, but he had a real and vital personal relationship with God. So, if God desired, He could tell those interpretations to Joseph.

Two years later, Pharaoh had two dreams, and no one could interpret them. The cupbearer told Pharaoh of a young Hebrew man he'd met in prison who had interpreted his and the baker's dreams and that everything he'd said would happen came to pass. Pharaoh had Joseph brought to him. He said to Joseph, "I had a dream, and no one can interpret it. But I have heard it said of you that when you hear a dream you can interpret it" (Gen. 41:15). Then Joseph surprised the king and said, "I cannot do it . . . but God will give Pharaoh the answer he desires" (v. 16).

Joseph knew that it was God working the miracles of perfect interpretations, not him. This is not a small distinction or a difference in semantics. It is a critical truth: God performs the miracles; we don't. But we can position ourselves to experience God's miracles, and we can open our spiritual eyes to see them.

> We can position ourselves to experience God's miracles, and we can open our spiritual eyes to see them.

However, some of the miracles He performs through us or around us have nothing to do with our positioning ourselves. Joseph didn't position himself into slavery or into prison—God worked all of the necessary circumstances for that to happen. As we saw in the previous chapter, Joseph merely had to position himself near enough to God to receive His favor and interpretations. Then he had to step out in faith and articulate the interpretations that he believed God had given him.

To go from the most cherished son of twelve to a teenage slave in a foreign country would cause almost anyone to feel that the God they had believed in was either uncaring or nonexistent. If you had gone from being the most cherished of all your siblings to a slave in a foreign country, what would you believe? Knowing myself, I'd probably pray like crazy for a while (maybe the first few weeks or months), and then I'd probably give up.

Joseph Principle #6: Expecting God to Work His Miracles Through Your Faith

And then, even worse, what would we believe about God if we refused to fall to temptation and as a result were thrown into prison—if we made the choice that honored God and, instead of rewarding us, He let us be imprisoned on false charges? I can't imagine having a faith that would get me past that one. Yet that's exactly the kind of faith Joseph had in the God of his father. Joseph not only still believed that God existed but had faith that the God he had learned about from his youth still possessed all of the amazing attributes he had been taught about. And he believed that his God was sovereign over the affairs of his life—as a slave, as a prisoner, and as a servant of Pharaoh. As stated in Joseph Principle #3, that firm belief in God's sovereignty and love was the very core of Joseph's amazing faith.

When we consider Joseph's faith, we think, *Of course God blessed him!* We could also think, *But I could never have that much faith!* Certainly, Jesus' disciples thought the same thing for most of their three and a half years with Jesus. They didn't even have enough faith to obey the simplest command from Christ. When Jesus told them they must forgive one another seven times in the same day, they cried out to the Lord,

"Increase our faith!" (Luke 17:5). Their problem wasn't that they didn't have enough faith. Their problem was that they didn't have *any* faith for that command. Jesus told them that with even the tiniest amount of faith they could say to a tree, **"Be uprooted and planted in the sea,"** and it would be done (v. 6). He was really telling them that if they had even the tiniest amount of faith, they would have said, "Yes, Lord—if you want us to forgive that often, we have the faith to obey your command."

My friend, we are often in the same boat as the disciples. When it comes to obeying Jesus, if we don't obey, our problem isn't too little faith, it's no faith in that particular moment for that particular situation. Even the tiniest amount of faith provides everything we need to hear His words and do them (Luke 6:47). Like the disciples prior to His resurrection, we simply don't have the faith to obey. Don't beat yourself up—this has been the struggle of every believer in history, to one degree or another. The question is whether it's possible for us to gain a faith like Joseph's. Answer: yes!

How to Receive the Faith God Wants Us to Have

Most believers I've known (including me) have often thought, *I wish I had more faith.* When I saw God heal my son of cancer through the faith of a pastor, I wished I had the level of faith he had. Have you ever cried out to the Lord, "Increase my faith"? That's exactly what I did after I saw God's miraculous deliverance of my son on the day of his operation.

In Mark 9 Jesus told a grieving father of a son who was demon possessed, **"Everything is possible for one who believes"** (v. 23). The boy's father immediately exclaimed, "I do believe; help me overcome my unbelief!" (v. 24). The man's plea was a wonderfully transparent reflection of his heart. It was also amazingly insightful. Have you ever felt the same way? So many times I've thought, *Of course I believe in God and the Lord*

101

Jesus, but I also see my unbelief. And that unbelief limits my vision, attitudes, and behavior in specific situations. Even if I don't pray those specific words, my feelings are, "Lord, help my unbelief."

We see this kind of faith dilemma many times in the lives of the disciples. They had enough faith in Christ to leave their families and livelihoods to follow Him nearly 24/7 for three and a half years. But they didn't have the faith to obey His commands to always forgive and never judge. They didn't have the faith to believe they would survive a stormy sea unless they woke Him up. In a panic they woke Him and pleaded, "Teacher, don't you care if we drown?" (Mark 4:38). Jesus instantly calmed the sea and then asked them, **"Why are you so afraid? Do you still have no faith?"** (v. 40). I can tell you right now, I not only sympathize with the disciples, but I would have done the same thing they did.

To their credit, they had enough faith to believe Jesus could save them if they woke Him up, but they did not have enough faith to believe that His mere presence in the boat would keep them safe, even though He was asleep. Then, when He calmed the storm with a simple three-word command, they were shocked and couldn't believe He was able to perform the miracle He had just performed. Once again, this was a situation that could be described by the father's dilemma of belief and unbelief in Mark 9. The disciples believed to the point they thought Jesus could do something but not to the point that His mere presence guaranteed their safety, certainly not to the point of believing He could control the weather and the sea with His words.

The question is not how we increase our faith but how we gain the type of faith we can use to replace our belief/unbelief dilemma. Once again, Jesus has the answer. But before we look at it, let's clarify what faith is and what it is not. Faith is not a feeling; it is a fully embraced persuasion in one's heart that always produces an attitude or action that expresses that persuasion.

Personally, to wrap my brain around this critical topic, I classify faith into two categories: general and specific. For example, I have a *general* faith that God exists and is loving, just, and righteous. This aspect of faith is based on what I've read in the Bible and on my personal experience in my relationship with Jesus throughout my life. My general faith produces a foundational peace, joy, and confidence in God the Father, the Son, and the Holy Spirit. It gives me a hunger to know Him more intimately. It produces gratefulness when I rightfully attribute everything I value to Him. This is not the type of faith that moves mountains that Jesus was referring to (Matt. 17:20) or that God often channels His miraculous works through.

Specific faith is basing a specific action or an attitude on a word from God that applies to a specific situation in a specific moment. The word from God comes first, and then faith takes a step on that word.

Specific Faith Requires a Word from God, Then You Take the Step of Obedience to God's Word or Command

Nearly every faith-based miracle recorded in the Gospels started with a statement or command from Jesus. Wisely, Peter would not step out of the boat onto the water until he received a command from Jesus. Seeing Jesus walking on the water, Peter cried out, "Lord, if it is You, command me to come to You on the water" (Matt. 14:28 NKJV). Peter knew that if Jesus commanded him to come, He would give him the grace, the power, the miracle to walk on the water.

Jesus gave him the one-word command, "**Come**" (v. 29). Now, all Peter had to do was obey the command—step out of the boat by faith. He wasn't stepping onto the water; he was stepping onto the command of Christ. The only faith he needed was to take the first step of obedience.

Step by step, Peter walked by faith. Each step he took reinforced his faith and gave him the courage to take the next step of faith. Then the wind kicked up and took his mind off Jesus' word, and his faith in the command of Christ was overcome and supplanted by his fear of sinking. Of course when he replaced his faith in Jesus' command with the fear of his circumstances, sink he did. He cried out to Jesus to save him, and Jesus reached down and pulled him out of the water (vv. 29–31).

Then Jesus said to him, "**You of little faith, why did you doubt?**" (v. 31 NKJV).

Unlike his zero faith to obey Jesus' command to forgive seven times, this time Peter had faith. He had enough faith to obey Jesus' command to come and miraculously walk on water, but his faith was little, because when the circumstance changed, he focused on the wind and replaced his faith with doubt. Notice Jesus' command didn't change, but Peter's faith was supplanted by doubt. That's why Jesus called his faith "little."

Examples of Faith-Based Obedience to Jesus' Word

- Jesus told the young man who was born blind to go wash his eyes in the pool of Siloam.
  - → He obeyed and received his sight (John 9).
- Jesus told His disciples to throw their nets to the other side of the boat.
  - → They obeyed and caught so many fish, their nets couldn't hold them (John 21:6).
- Jesus told the man whose daughter had just died, "**Don't be afraid; just believe.**"
  - → The father chose to ignore his friends and believe Jesus' command, and his daughter came back to life (Mark 5:36–42).
- Jesus told Lazarus's sisters to remove the stone blocking Lazarus's tomb.
  - → They ordered the stone removed, and Lazarus came back to life (John 11:38–44).

- Jesus told the servants to fill the empty water jars with water.
  - → They obeyed, and more than 120 gallons of water were turned into wine (John 2:6–10).
- Jesus told the man who had been sick for thirty-eight years to get up and walk.
  - → He obeyed Jesus' command, and after thirty-eight years of incapacitating illness, he was healed (John 5:8–9).
- Jesus told the paralyzed man, "Get up, take your mat and go home."
  - → He obeyed, and life and strength came back to his body and his paralysis disappeared (Matt. 9:6).

The Great Faith That Shocked Jesus

Jesus had just come into the town of Capernaum when a Roman army commander came up to Him. "Lord," he said, "my servant lies at home paralyzed, suffering terribly" (Matt. 8:6).

Jesus graciously asked, **"Shall I come and heal him?"** (v. 7).

The commander replied, "Lord, I do not deserve to have you come under my roof. But just say the word, and my servant will be healed. For I myself am a man under authority, with soldiers under me. I tell this one, 'Go,' and he goes; and that one, 'Come,' and he comes. I say to my servant, 'Do this,' and he does it" (vv. 8–9).

Wow! Everyone else who had ever pressed Jesus for a miracle believed He had to be physically present to perform it. As we saw, Jesus' disciples even thought that He not only had to be present but had to be awake. And when He calmed the storm and the sea with three words, they were shocked again.

Not the commander. His faith wasn't little; it was giant! He realized that Jesus wasn't like a doctor who had to make a personal visit to heal a person. His faith was way outside that box! He still needed a word to base his faith on, but he didn't need Jesus to even make a house call. All he needed was a spoken word. He saw Jesus as much more than a man. He saw him as a miracle worker who wasn't limited by time or distance. He likely believed Jesus was indeed divine, because only God could speak a command in one place that would miraculously heal someone far away in another place.

This isn't just amazing to me. It shocked and amazed Jesus too. We're told, "When Jesus heard this, he was amazed and said to those following him, '**Truly I tell you, I have not found anyone in Israel with such great faith**'" (Matt. 8:10). A few moments later Jesus looked at the commander and said, "**Go! Let it be done just as you believed it would**" (v. 13). We are told that the commander's servant was healed at that precise moment (v. 13).

Yes, Miracles Still Happen

We see that miracles require two ingredients: a word or command from Jesus and faith to obey that word or command. "Wait a minute," you say. "How am I supposed to get a specific word or command from Jesus for the specific situations I encounter?" If that is really your question, as we saw in the last chapter, Jesus has already given you all of the specific commands and words you need to step out in faith in any situation you encounter. The more than eighty conditional promises He gave, along with the 150 commands, are all gifts from Jesus Himself to empower you to act by faith and obey. This is how we grow our faith. Anytime you obey Jesus' words in any situation, you are not only using His love language, you are expressing faith. Paul told us we are to "walk by faith, not by sight" (2 Cor. 5:7 NASB), and hearing and doing what Jesus said is how we walk by faith. This also grows our faith. This is what Paul meant when he wrote, "So faith comes from hearing, and hearing by the word of Christ" (Rom. 10:17 NASB).

In banking terms, God expresses His grace by making deposits of Jesus' words into our minds and hearts. We then have the choice—we

> Anytime you obey Jesus' words in any situation, you are not only using His love language; you are expressing faith.

can ignore His deposits and live like spiritual paupers, or we can believe Jesus' words and exercise faith by acting on them. Faith is writing checks on the deposits God has made. God has made those deposits at the bank of Jesus' words—the Gospels. We go to that bank and transfer God's deposits from the four gospel accounts into our account (our mind and heart).

How can you see more miracles in your life? Whether you're eight years old or eighty, the answer is the same. Discover the commands, teachings, and promises of Jesus' words in the Gospels and begin to take steps of faith, acting on His words. The miracles He promises will follow you. They will surround your life every day as you walk by faith. He gives the words, you take the steps. It's that easy.

In the last chapter, we looked at Matthew 11:28–30 to see how Jesus' commands can be applied to our trials and heartaches. It provides such a great example of how we can use such conditional promises to act in faith, I want to take one more look at it from this perspective.

Example: Matthew 11:28–30

Come to me, all you who are weary and burdened, and I will give you rest. Take my yoke upon you and learn from me, for I am gentle and humble in heart, and you will find rest for your souls. For my yoke is easy and my burden is light.

Here Jesus gives us three commands and the promises that are conditioned on those commands.

Commands

- Come to Me when you are weary (worn out or stressed) and are weighed down with a burden.
- Learn from Me.
- Take My yoke upon you.

Promised Benefits

- You will receive relief from your stress and burdens.
- He will teach you with humility and gentleness.
- You will receive relief and physical refreshment, not superficially but all the way down to the depths of your soul.
- His commands are not burdensome—they don't add weight to your burden.

Faith-Based Obedient Actions

- Come to Jesus and His words first, before you go to anyone else.
- Read and learn from His words.
- Base your attitude and behavior on His words and teachings. (That's what it means to take on His rabbinical yoke.)

As we saw in the previous chapter, Jesus is referring to His rabbinical yoke. While other rabbis' yokes added burdensome commands to the law, making it too hard to bear, Jesus said that His yoke was just the opposite—it lightened people's burdens instead of adding to them. Instead of weighing you down, Jesus' teachings and commands in the Gospels become like helium in a balloon. They empower you to soar above your burdens and into His miraculous living.

The Dividing Line Between a Life That Stands and a Life That Collapses

Jesus' words not only provide the specific words we need to walk by faith; according to Jesus, they are the difference between a life that will or will not withstand the trials and adversities we encounter. They are even the difference between an eternity spent with Christ and an eternity spent without Him. Jesus' words provide the firm foundation of our assurance that we have indeed been born of the Spirit. Jesus ended His Sermon on the Mount with a startling revelation of professing believers discovering that He had never had an intimate relationship with them. He said, "**Not everyone who says to Me, 'Lord, Lord,' will enter the kingdom of heaven, but the one who does the will of My Father who is in heaven will enter. Many will say to Me on that day, 'Lord, Lord, did we not prophesy in Your name, and in Your name cast out demons, and in Your name perform many miracles?' And then I will declare to them, 'I never knew you; leave Me, you who practice lawlessness'**" (Matt. 7:21–23 NASB).

For more than forty years, this passage really bothered me. The people Jesus is referring to here really thought they were doing what He wanted them to do. And then He shocked them with His pronouncement that He never knew them and commanded them to depart from His presence. I always thought, *Yikes, what if I'm included in that group?*

Then, in 2005, I didn't stop at verse 23 but kept reading. The next verse begins a new paragraph, but it starts with the word *Therefore*. That means the whole point of verses 21 through 23 is what He's going to reveal in verses 24 through 27. He said,

> **Therefore, everyone who hears these words of Mine, and acts on them, will be like a wise man who built his house on the rock. And the rain fell and the floods came, and the winds blew and slammed against that**

house; and yet it did not fall, for it had been founded on the rock. And everyone who hears these words of Mine, and does not act on them, will be like a foolish man who built his house on the sand. And the rain fell and the floods came, and the winds blew and slammed against that house; and it fell—and its collapse was great. (NASB)

Here's the dividing line that Jesus Himself declared. As He explained, the "rock" is hearing His words and doing what He says, while the "sand" is hearing His words and not doing what He says.

Going back to our earlier example, you heard His commands to come to Him when you're stressed, weary, and burdened, to learn from Him and take His yoke upon you. Next time you're really stressed, weary, or burdened, you have a choice: obey His words in Matthew 11:28–30 or don't obey them. If you obey them, you're taking steps of faith, loving Him and the Father using Their love language, and you will receive His miraculous promises from that passage. If you don't obey them, you're not acting in faith, not taking the opportunity to love God with His love language, and not guaranteed His miraculous promises in that passage. Also, when you obey, you're building your life on the rock, and if you don't, you're building your life on the sand.

> When you obey, you're building your life on the rock, and if you don't, you're building your life on the sand.

How Do You Find God's Deposits and Transfer Them to Your Heart?

Jesus said, "The words I have spoken to you—they are full of the Spirit and life" (John 6:63). When we meditate on His words and do what they say, they infuse His Spirit and life into our spirit and life. God's trillion-dollar bank account of promises is housed in the Gospels. He is waiting to transfer those promises into your faith account. And the transferring process isn't complicated. We read His words, ponder them, pray about them, and then we step out in faith—we act on them and obey them. A great place to start is the Sermon on the Mount (Matt. 5–7). Of course, the Gospel of John is another great place to start. All four gospels contain Christ's amazing teachings, commands, and promises. Remember, faith is not positive thinking, it's not a ritual, it's not an abstract mystical experience. Faith is tangible. It requires a word, a saying, a teaching, a command, or a promise from the Word of God in general, but more specifically, from the spoken words of Jesus. These deposits are waiting for you. Now's the time to dive into Jesus' glorious words!

In addition to the Gospels, Jesus' promises are easily found in *Greatest Words Ever Spoken*, pages 299–304, under the topic *The Promises of Christ*.

Joseph Principle #6: Expecting God to Work His Miracles Through Your Faith

Chapter 8

HOW TO FORGIVE
EVEN WHEN YOU
DON'T FEEL LIKE IT

For if you forgive other people when they sin
against you, your heavenly Father will also
forgive you. But if you do not forgive others their
sins, your Father will not forgive your sins.

Matthew 6:14–15

While Potiphar, the prison warden, and Pharaoh knew that God was
with Joseph because of his extraordinary, unexplainable success,
I know that God was with Joseph because of the amazing, unimaginable
forgiveness he freely extended to his brothers. He not only forgave them;
he loved them and committed himself to take care of them and all of their
families for the rest of their lives. No one could ever sincerely and freely

forgive the level of evil they had committed against Joseph—unless they were intimately related to God.

C. S. Lewis wrote, "Everyone thinks forgiveness is a lovely idea, until he has something to forgive."[1] He also wrote, "To be a Christian means to forgive the inexcusable because God has forgiven the inexcusable in you."[2] In my many years as a follower of Christ, every Christian I have known believes it is the obligation of every believer, including themselves, to forgive those who offend them. Yet it takes only a few minutes of asking the right questions to discover that nearly every believer has someone they are struggling to forgive.

_____

Joseph Principle #7: Forgiving Others Because God Forgives Us

_____

Occasionally, extending forgiveness is easy when the offense is minor and the offender is someone we dearly love. But usually, forgiving seems terribly difficult or even impossible. In fact, more often than not, forgiving a major offense, or what C. S. Lewis calls "the inexcusable," requires a miracle. To forgive the unforgivable, a miraculous transformation must take place within our heart.

Understanding What True Forgiveness Is and What It Is Not

There is a great deal of misunderstanding on what true forgiveness is and what it is not. Even though feelings may have kept us from forgiving someone, the truth is that feelings have nothing to do with the kind of forgiveness Jesus talked about. Forgiveness is not a feeling. It is a specific action or behavior taken by the victim toward the offender. Something I learned at a Gary Smalley seminar was the Aramaic word that Jesus used is *shavaq*. It literally means "to untie and release." It implies the act of granting a full pardon. Both the Hebrew word and Greek word also imply the act of pardoning. To forgive someone is to untie them from their obligation to you for their offensive actions toward you or those you care about. You are literally granting them a full pardon from their sin(s) against you. In granting this

> To forgive someone is to untie them from their obligation to you for their offensive actions toward you or those you care about.

pardon, you are releasing them from any and all obligations to you that their sins created.

Forgiveness does not mean that you restore them to the place of trust or affection that you formerly experienced with them. That is reconciliation, and reconciliation is an issue altogether different from forgiveness. You may or may not choose to reconcile. To reconcile, there must be a significant change in attitude and behavior so that trust may be restored. Forgiveness, by contrast, is merely a release of obligation. While forgiveness does not necessarily involve a restoration of trust or emotional feelings, reconciliation usually does. Also, when you forgive someone, you can forgive them only for what they have done to you. You can pardon them from their debt and obligation to you, but you cannot release them from their debt or obligation to others, including society if their offense included a crime.

Forgiveness Unties the Offender from You and You from Them

Forgiving the offender not only grants them a full pardon; it unties them from you. When you don't forgive an offender, they remain tied to you, and you remain tied to them. That means that if they drive over a spiritual cliff, they pull you over that same cliff. If they are driven by self-centeredness, you, too, will find yourself dragged into self-centeredness. If they move deeper into a godless life, they will drag you deeper into a godless life. But when you forgive them, you not only untie them from you but untie yourself from them. You are no longer a slave or even subject to anything they do.

One of my neighbors defrauded me out of my entire life savings. It had taken me twenty-three years to earn that savings, and it was all gone within a couple of months. When I understood the true meaning of forgiveness, I very quickly forgave him. I knew he would never have the ability to pay me back, and by forgiving him I was releasing him from all of his sin debt and his financial obligation to me. However, I will never again enter into a business relationship with him that would require me to trust him. Years later, when he was jailed for defrauding someone else in another state, I sincerely prayed for him. When he came home and came to church, I joyfully and sincerely welcomed him home. When he was later struck with cancer, I prayed for him. When he miraculously survived his terminal diagnosis, I hugged him and rejoiced with him and his family. He is still a friend I love, and I pray for his growth in his relationship with the Lord.

Thankfully, God replaced some of the money he took from me with money from my other projects. I'm not sharing this to convey in any way that I am superspiritual. I'm not even close to being the person I want to be. But I share this to show that our feelings of grief, hurt, and betrayal do not have to prevent us from forgiving anyone.

Forgiveness Is Not Optional for Followers of Jesus—It's Mandatory

In the last chapter we saw Jesus' disciples panic when He told them that they must forgive a person as many as seven times for the same offense in the same day. When they pleaded for more faith, Jesus revealed that when it came to obeying His command to forgive, they had no faith. Later, Peter decided to double-check Jesus' teaching on forgiveness. He came up to Jesus and asked, "Lord, how many times shall my brother sin against me and I still forgive him? Up to seven times?" (Matt. 18:21 NASB). Jesus said to him, "**I do not say to you, up to seven times, but up to seventy times seven**" (v. 22 NKJV).

Peter was finally getting comfortable with Jesus' command to forgive seven times when Jesus decimated his comfort zone with an even more impossible command: 7 times 70, or 490. Sensing Peter's absolute dismay, Jesus gave him an amazing parable—a parable that would not only show Peter *why* he should and must forgive but, more specifically, *how* he could forgive. In this parable Jesus also shows you and me *why* we must forgive and *how* we, too, can forgive. Jesus said,

> For this reason the kingdom of heaven is like a king who wanted to settle accounts with his slaves. And when he had begun to settle them, one who owed him ten thousand talents was brought to him. But since he did not have the means to repay, his master commanded that he be sold, along with his wife and children and all that he had, and repayment be made. So the slave fell to the ground and prostrated himself before him, saying, 'Have patience with me and I will repay you everything.' And the master of that slave felt compassion, and he released him and forgave him the debt. But that slave went out and found one of his fellow slaves who owed him a hundred denarii; and he seized him and began to choke him, saying, 'Pay back what you owe!' So his fellow slave fell to the ground and began to plead with him, saying, 'Have patience with me and I will repay you.' But he was unwilling, and went and threw him in prison until he would pay back what was owed. So when his fellow slaves saw what had happened, they were deeply grieved and came and reported to their master all that had

happened. Then summoning him, his master said to him, 'You wicked slave, I forgave you all that debt because you pleaded with me. Should you not also have had mercy on your fellow slave, in the same way that I had mercy on you?' And his master, moved with anger, handed him over to the torturers until he would repay all that was owed him. My heavenly Father will also do the same to you, if each of you does not forgive his brother from your heart. (Matt. 18:23–35 NASB)

The first thing that should be noted is that ten thousand talents was an enormously large amount of money—nearly $4 billion in today's dollars. It would equal about sixty million days of labor. On the other hand, one hundred denarii would equal about one hundred days of labor.[3] The man who was forgiven an amount of debt that was impossible to even conceive of, much less pay back, refused to forgive an amount that by comparison was almost nothing. Even worse, he threw his debtor into prison. His actions were not only merciless; they were ruthless. Even more disgusting, his actions demonstrated to everyone (his fellow laborers and his boss) that he had no appreciation, no gratefulness at all for the incredible mercy he had been shown.

Our Why for Forgiving

Thus, in this parable Jesus is telling Peter and you and me that because God has forgiven us such an enormous, impossible-to-repay debt, how dare we not forgive the minuscule sin debt others inflict on us. God not only forgave us for every bad thought, attitude, and deed we've ever committed: He sacrificed His only Son to pay off our impossible sin debt. Jesus, in obedience to His Father, suffered through the humiliation of a fraudulent trial, an excruciating scourging, and the absolute worst form of capital punishment—crucifixion. Why? Because He loved His

Father and He loved His sheep. In this parable, Jesus was telling us that God's inconceivable act of forgiveness, sacrifice, and mercy is the reason we must forgive. He was telling us that no other reason is needed. His forgiveness of us is the "why" for our forgiving others.

Not Extending Forgiveness Reveals a Critical Flaw in Our Understanding

The Great Escape

My father was a bomber pilot in World War II. On one of his missions, after releasing their bombs, his plane got separated from his squadron's formation, and he was starting the trek back to his base alone. He said from out of nowhere a formation of twelve enemy fighters swarmed his plane. His aircraft didn't stand a chance. The other fighters were faster, more maneuverable, and outnumbered his plane twelve to one. He knew that he and his nine crew members were going to die. They had no hope. His plane got hit again and again by enemy aircraft machine guns.

Then, from out of the blue, an Australian fighter came into the fray. In less than two minutes, the fighter pilot shot down three of the enemy fighters. Dad said he had never seen anything like it. After downing three of the fighters, the remaining nine decided they were no match for this crazy Aussie. They turned away from my dad's plane and started their retreat. Dad said the Aussie didn't stop. He kept chasing the nine and continually engaged them, likely downing a few more.

My dad's plane, though badly shot up, limped back to the base. He told me, "Steve, we were truly doomed. We had absolutely no hope—*none*! And then came the Aussie. One plane against twelve, and he saved us. He *saved* us!"

There was a time when you and I, like my dad, were in a terrible life-and-death situation. In fact, in Ephesians 2:1, Paul told us that we were actually dead. Our sins and violations of God's laws had left us spiritually dead with no hope of gaining eternal life or even having any spiritual connection with God. Paul said in verse 12 that we were in the world, having no hope. *Dead* means no life and no chance of living at all—*none*! When you're dead, there's no rewind, no second chances—in fact, no chances at all. Your life is gone, all gone, and nothing can save you. You're dead. As bleak as this is, this was our true spiritual condition—dead, with no hope.

"I'm Not *That* Bad!"

When you compare yourselves to others, you really aren't that bad. Being dead in sin doesn't mean you're as bad as Adolf Hitler. It means you are spiritually dead (permanently separated from God) as evidenced by your self-centered nature and the selfishness and sin that flow from that nature. Compared to God, whose character is as white as snow, your character is as black as coal.

When King David saw the greatness of his sins in contrast to God's perfect righteousness, he cried out to God, "My sin is ever before me" (Ps. 51:3 ESV). In other words, his sins surrounded him like an ocean of sharks around a drowning swimmer. When the apostle Paul looked at his failings compared to God's righteousness, he cried out, "O wretched man that I am! Who will deliver me from this body of death?" (Rom. 7:24 NKJV).

In Luke 18, Jesus gave a parable of the contrast between a self-righteous Pharisee and a lowly tax collector. The Pharisee went into the temple and prayed, telling God that he fasted twice a week and gave a tenth of his income. The tax collector, on the other hand, didn't feel he was worthy enough to even go into the temple. He stayed outside and didn't even feel worthy enough to look toward heaven. Looking down, he beat his chest and simply cried in anguish, "God, be merciful to me, the sinner!" (v. 13 NASB). Jesus said the lowly tax collector went home justified before God. The Pharisee did not (vv. 9–14).

David, Paul, and of course the lowly tax collector saw the absolute hopelessness of their sinful plight. Their only hope was that God would have mercy on them. And then came Jesus. Like the Aussie pilot that saved my dad from his hopeless peril, his sure death, God's one and only Son was sent to rescue you and me. One Son against the devil himself and his billions of demons. One Son to rescue not just you and me but millions of men, women, boys, and girls—all who would trust Him—from their hopeless, self-centered life and spiritual death. Paul wrote, "But because of his great love for us, God, who is rich in mercy, made us alive with Christ even when we were dead in transgressions—it is by grace you have been saved" (Eph. 2:4–5).

Though our sins made us red as scarlet, through Jesus, God made us white as snow. That's what God Himself told Isaiah when He said, "'Come now, and let us reason together,' says the LORD, 'Though your sins are like scarlet, they shall be as white as snow; though they are red like crimson, they shall be as wool'" (Isa. 1:18 NKJV).

Paul wrote, "There is therefore now no condemnation to those who are in Christ Jesus" (Rom. 8:1 NKJV). He also wrote, "But God proves His love for us in this: While we were still sinners, Christ died for us" (Rom. 5:8 BSB). Then, in 2 Corinthians 5:21, Paul wrote, "God made Him who knew no sin to be sin on our behalf, so that in Him we might become the righteousness of God" (BSB). So even though you and I were dead in sin, God gave us a spiritual birth that made us alive in Christ. He took all of our sins and failings and put them on Christ, and He put Jesus' perfect righteousness—the very righteousness of God—on us. Jesus not only rescued us from spiritual death and made us spiritually alive, but He also cleansed us from all of our unrighteousness and made us white as snow. This is why we must forgive. Our salvation, and all that it entails, is the greatest and most costly miracle God has ever performed. When we forgive, we are expressing the gratitude that the Father and Son so aptly deserve.

"Rejoice That Your Names Are Recorded in Heaven"

In the Gospel of Luke, we see that the disciples were amazed by the signs and miracles Jesus performed and by the miracles they performed in His name. In the tenth chapter of Luke, Jesus sent out seventy-two men (including His twelve disciples) and gave them the authority to perform miracles and cast out demons. When they returned, we are told they rejoiced and said, "Lord, even the demons are subject to us in Your name" (v. 17 NKJV). After making a comment, Jesus told them, **"Nevertheless, do not rejoice in this, that the spirits are subject to you, but rejoice that your names are recorded in heaven"** (v. 20 NASB). In other words, experiencing the miracles they did was good, but the real reason to rejoice was the greatest miracle of all—their salvation. Their salvation and ours were not only God's greatest miracles, but they were also the only miracles that cost God something. It cost the terrible price of His only Son's sacrifice on the cross.

> The real reason to rejoice was the greatest miracle of all— their salvation.

Later, after Jesus' resurrection, they finally understood the magnitude and magnificence of the forgiveness God had given them and His incomparable gift of eternal life. That is the gospel, the good news that drove them and their message for the rest of their lives.

Understanding the Magnitude of God's Forgiveness Increases Your Love for Him

A Pharisee named Simon invited Jesus to dinner at his home. As Jesus reclined at the table, a woman who was known for her sinful lifestyle entered the home and positioned herself by His feet. Her heart was broken by her overwhelming sense of personal guilt and shame. But I believe the brokenness she felt from her guilt and shame wasn't the only feeling she was experiencing as she drew near Jesus. I believe she could feel the love and mercy that seemed to freely flow from Him. Seeing His manner and hearing His voice, she could sense His flawless purity, and that magnified even more the contrast between His holiness and her sinfulness. Yet, unlike the disdain and judgment she had always felt from others, she felt no judgment from Him. From Him she felt empathy and compassion like she had never known.

As she wept, her tears wet Jesus' feet. She then wiped His feet with her hair and kissed His feet as she poured a very expensive perfumed oil on them. As she continued, Simon thought, *If this man were a prophet, he would know who is touching him and what kind of woman she is—that she is a sinner.*

Jesus perceived what Simon was thinking and said to him,

> **"Two people owed money to a certain moneylender. One owed him five hundred denarii, and the other fifty. Neither of them had the money to pay him back, so he forgave the debts of both. Now which of them will love him more?"**
>
> Simon replied, "I suppose the one who had the bigger debt forgiven."
>
> **"You have judged correctly,"** Jesus said. (Luke 7:41–43)

In this parable, Jesus was saying that the person who knows they've been forgiven the greatest debt loves the most. He underscored this with His actions and words that followed. He turned toward the woman and said to Simon, **"Do you see this woman? I came into your house. You did not give me any water for my feet, but she wet my feet with her tears and wiped them with her hair. You did not give me a kiss, but this woman, from the time I entered, has not stopped kissing my feet. You did not put** oil on my head, but she has poured perfume on my feet. Therefore, I tell you, her many sins have been forgiven—as her great love has shown. But whoever has been forgiven little loves little" (Luke 7:44–47).

"Whoever Has Been Forgiven Little Forgives Little"

This parable not only reveals that those who have been forgiven little love little but also reveals the first and greatest obstacle that prevents us from forgiving others. That obstacle is our failure to understand the enormity of the problem our sin creates in relation to our chances of ever gaining eternal life and intimacy with a perfectly holy and righteous God. Most people, like the Pharisee, truly believe that their sins aren't really that bad. We are quick to compare ourselves to people we know or have heard about that seem to be a lot worse than us. Consequently, we tend to view our salvation as little more than a religious rite of passage. And since we don't view our sins as that horrific, when we hear that they are forgiven, it doesn't strike us as being that big of deal. Jesus said, "**Whoever has been forgiven little loves little**," and we can just as easily say, "Whoever has been forgiven little *forgives* little." Anyone who finds it hard to forgive someone has not come into the true realization of how much God has forgiven of them.

The first step to discovering the joy and the ease of forgiving someone else is to gain a more accurate picture of the greatest miracle of your life—your miraculous rescue from being separated from God for eternity.

Choosing Not to Forgive Mocks God and Belittles Jesus' Sacrifice

Not to forgive demonstrates that we don't understand or appreciate how much we've been forgiven. It reveals that we don't understand the enormity of our sin debt. We grossly undervalue what the cancellation of our impossible sin debt cost God and His dear Son. Our refusal to forgive belittles and mocks the magnitude of God's love and mercy and Jesus' sacrifice. Choosing not to forgive someone is as displeasing to God as those who were mocking and spitting on His Son on the cross. It shows an extraordinary lack of gratefulness, and it reveals that we have never realized the depth of our own hopelessness and the incomprehensible size of our sin debt. It shows that we have never realized the Mount Everest magnitude of the Father's and the Son's love and mercy toward us.

Through the parable of the two debtors, Jesus clearly and emphatically demonstrates that our "why" for forgiving others has nothing to do with their sin toward us—but everything to do with our sin toward God and the eternal forgiveness He extends to us. So, we forgive others, not because they deserve it, but because it is a glorious way we can love God and show our gratefulness to Him. That's our "why."

> We forgive others because it is a glorious way we can love God and show our gratefulness to Him.

Why Our Feelings Can Make It So Hard to Forgive

God created us with a glorious capacity to experience emotions. He created us in His image (Gen. 1:27), and He, too, has emotions. We can see them expressed in the Old Testament,[4] and we see Jesus' emotions expressed throughout His life. Even while hanging on the cross, He expressed His love and care for His mother and His forgiveness for us and the very people who nailed Him to the cross. Yes, God created us with the capacity to feel. Experiencing feelings of emotional pain, joy, love, grief, or sorrow can empower us to become kinder and more compassionate, merciful, understanding, and loving of others. Unfortunately, we can also allow our emotions to shape destructive attitudes and drive our hurtful behavior. Tragically, our emotions often become our master.

When we are hurt by another person's offense against us, if we don't quickly resolve that hurt with forgiveness, it gives birth to anger, bitterness, and resentment. And when we bury our hurt instead of resolving it, like the magma inside a volcano, it can burn us up inside and change who we are for the worse. Whether we express our anger or bury it, our feelings can become our master, and because we don't feel like forgiving, we don't. Jesus said, **"No one can serve two masters. Either you will hate the one and love the other, or you will be devoted to the one and despise the other"** (Matt. 6:24). In light of Jesus' numerous commands to forgive, when we do not forgive, we remove Him from the ruling throne of our hearts and replace Him with unforgiveness and its accompanying anger, resentment, and bitterness. We are replacing Jesus as the Master of our lives with our own self-centeredness and the feelings of unforgiveness that we harbor. Sadly, even when we want to forgive, our feelings won't let us.

Obstacles That Can Block Our Forgiving

As my son Sean and I discussed forgiveness, I asked him, "What do you think are the big obstacles that can prevent a follower of Christ from forgiving someone?" Our quick list was the following.

Obstacles That Prevent People from Forgiving Others
- Self-centeredness
- Pride
- Wanting "justice"

- Believing the offender doesn't deserve to be forgiven
- Wanting the other person to repent first
- Emotional hurt that won't go away
- Not understanding what forgiveness is
- Simply not knowing how to forgive

Take a moment to look at this list and make check marks by the obstacles that you think have kept you from forgiving someone. All of these are legitimate reasons for an unbeliever not to forgive an offender. And these same reasons often keep believers from forgiving. However, as followers of Christ, none of these reasons have to prevent us from forgiving. Why? Because the Good Shepherd that we follow has commanded us to forgive. Remember, forgiving is the act of untying and releasing. Untying someone from their obligation to us has nothing to do with feelings. We forgive because we are commanded to do so, and when we do forgive, we are obeying this command of Jesus, and thus we are loving the Father and the Son, using Their love language of obeying Jesus' teachings.

Imagine where you would be if God used these same reasons as obstacles that prevented Him from forgiving you! Let's take a look.

God Decides He Won't Forgive You Because . . .

- **He's too concerned about Himself.** Imagine Him saying, "I created them and all they do is take advantage of Me. Woe is Me—I'm going to ignore them and just let them die."
- **Pride.** Imagine Him saying, "You rejected My Son's teachings so, to heck with you!"
- **Wanting justice.** He reminds Himself of how unrighteous and self-centered you are—and "the soul who sins shall die" (Ezek. 18:20 NKJV). Imagine Him saying, "They deserve eternal separation from Me, so that's just what I'm going to give them."
- **Believing the offender doesn't deserve to be forgiven.** Imagine

Him saying, "You don't deserve to be forgiven. You and your sins murdered My one and only Son!"

- **Wanting the other person to repent first**. Imagine Him saying, "Your repentance means nothing. Almost as soon as you repent, you turn around and sin again . . . and again and again and again."
- **Emotional hurt that won't go away**. Imagine Him saying, "You not only killed My Son, you continually break My heart by not hearing and doing what My Son said."
- **Not understanding what forgiveness is**. Imagine Him saying, "I don't *feel* like forgiving you, so I won't."
- **Simply not knowing how to forgive**. Imagine Him saying, "How can I possibly forgive you? You're such a mess, and you offend Me a hundred times a day. You're constantly doing what you shouldn't do and not doing what you should be doing."

Thankfully, none of these come even close to reflecting our awesome God and His beloved Son. In fact, they are truly 180 degrees opposite. Jesus proclaimed, **"For God so loved the world that he gave his one and only Son, that whoever believes in him shall not perish but have eternal life"** (John 3:16).

The Proactive Ways Jesus Gives Us to Express Our Forgiveness of Another

Remember, forgiving an offender is releasing them from their sin debt against us. It's the act of granting them a full pardon. Even more important, we are removing unforgiveness and the feelings of anger and resentment from the ruling throne of our hearts. Then, Jesus can take His rightful place as our Lord and Master. Jesus not only empowers us with all of the grace and faith we need to forgive our offenders, but He also gives us the grace to go above and beyond anything we, they, or the world could ever imagine. He gives us the grace to proactively love those we previously struggled to forgive.

"Wait a minute," you say. "Steve, you said that forgiving doesn't require feelings, and now you're telling me that Jesus wants me to love my offenders and enemies? How can that be?"

Yes, Jesus said, "**Love your enemies, do good to those who hate you, bless those who curse you, pray for those who mistreat you**" (Luke 6:27–28). But once again, as you will see, obeying these seemingly impossible commands has

> He gives us the grace to proactively love those we previously struggled to forgive.

nothing to do with our feelings. Rather, they refer entirely to our behavior. When you understand what Jesus is saying, you realize that these, too, are actions and behaviors—not feelings. We forgive others to show our love and gratitude for the Father and the Son giving us Their forgiveness and to return Jesus to the ruling throne of our hearts.

Four Ways to Express Forgiveness of Your Offenders

Luke 6:27–28 is one of the most quoted, most misunderstood, and even most scoffed-at passages in the Bible. Jesus was not giving these commands to nations or organizations. They were given as part of His Sermon on the Mount and were intended for His disciples—those who believed in Him and chose to follow Him by hearing and doing what He taught. These four commands are actions that wonderfully express forgiveness in a manner and to a degree that is not natural to us but is natural to the

Holy Spirit. As you forgive your offender, you not only allow Jesus to reclaim the throne of your heart but also provide the Holy Spirit with a channel to express what is natural to Him—the fruit of the Spirit, which includes God's amazing agape love. Let's look at them one at a time.

1. "Love Your Enemies"

As I mentioned, when Jesus instructs us to love our enemies, He is referring to *agape* love rather than *phileo* love. Phileo is a love that by nature involves affection. Agape love, on the other hand, involves the selfless love of God. It is not produced by our human nature but rather by the Holy Spirit. It is an action-based love rather than an affection-based love. The action proactively gives, and it often involves sacrificing. Often the one who agape loves sacrifices time, effort, and self-interest. It is the type of love Jesus speaks of throughout the Gospels. He uses it in John 3:16: **"For God so loved the world that he gave his one and only Son."** And of course, we see Jesus expressing agape every day of His life.

We experience this kind of love only when we are born of the Spirit (John 3:1–6). Agape love is the first fruit of the Spirit (Gal. 5:22). He produces that love in us, and we experience it as it flows through our hearts and minds to the person we are agape loving. In this command, Jesus was not demanding that we gain or express affection to our enemy but rather that we agape love them. How can we do that? We can pray for them, for their redemption and growth in their relationship with God. We can anonymously meet a genuine need. We can refuse to gossip about them or assail them to others. We are not expected or required to maintain any proximity that could produce physical or emotional harm. If all we do is pray for their redemption, we are agape loving them.

2. "Do Good to Those Who Hate You"

Like loving our enemies, this is a nearly impossible command to follow without the power and fruit of the Holy Spirit. Have you ever been hated? I have. There have been a few people in my life who hated me so much, I believe they truly wished me dead. Apart from a miracle, their hearts will never change. But I do all the good I can toward them—namely, I pray for them and their families and I muzzle my mouth to keep from telling others some of the horrible activities they have engaged in. Doing good in this case is not only doing positive things like praying for them; it's also a matter of not retaliating or doing things that could hurt them. A friend of mine who has similarly experienced this kind of hatred has anonymously left expensive boxes of candy at Christmas on the doorsteps of the very people who cheated him, lied about him, and tried to destroy him.

3. "Bless Those Who Curse You"

The Greek word translated "bless" is *eulogeo*. It is a verb that means "to invoke a blessing" or "to praise." It is the complete opposite of the word *curse*. The Greek word for "curse" means to invoke or pray for evil to befall someone. Here, Jesus is saying that when you think someone hates you enough to hope or pray that evil will come on you or even destroy you, you are to ask God to confer a tangible or spiritual blessing on that person. Of course, this, too, is not natural for any of us, but it expresses agape love, and therefore it is natural for the Holy Spirit. We can ask God to bless someone who hates us. Or, as a follower of Christ, we have the authority to pronounce a blessing on that person in Jesus' name. Either way, we will be loving God by obeying this command of our Lord and Savior.

Once again, we don't have to feel it to do it. We don't have to add feelings of affection to this act of invoking or pronouncing a blessing. We don't do it because the hateful person deserves it; rather, we do it in obedience to Christ, loving Him and the Father with God's love language.

4. "Pray for Those Who Mistreat You"

Here, Jesus is instructing us to pray for those who mistreat us. In the original language the word translated "mistreat" is a much stronger word that implies abuse and being despitefully manipulated or deceived. Once again, Jesus' instruction has nothing to do with feelings or affections. Also note that He's telling us to pray for the one who has despitefully used and abused us. He is not telling us to engage that person physically or emotionally. Prayer is something we can do from a safe distance, and our Good Shepherd wants to keep us away from the wolves that want to harm us. He loves His sheep. He loves us so much that He willingly laid down His life to save us (John 10:11–15). He doesn't lead us into harm's way, and He's not instructing us to be in proximity to abusers and risk harm to us or others.

Yes, He may lead us through "the darkest valley," and He may fellowship with us right in the presence of our enemies, but He protects us with His mighty rod and He rescues us with His compassionate staff (Ps. 23:4). Knowing that Jesus gives us these and other practical steps that we can take, without the need of our feeling love or affection for our offenders, enables us to follow our dear Savior's words and the examples of His life.

Joseph Principle #7: Forgiving Others Because God Forgives Us

Can You Think of Anyone You Haven't Forgiven?

Now it's your turn to put into practice your Good Shepherd's amazing teachings on forgiveness. You're not only going to release your offenders; you're going to untie yourself from them. In doing so, you'll be set free from the enslavement of the ruthless taskmaster of unforgiveness. Are you ready?

1. Name a person who you haven't been able to fully forgive.

   _____.

2. Pray.
   a. Tell the Father and the Lord Jesus how grateful you are for Their forgiveness.
   b. Thank the Father for His amazing love, that He would send His Son to experience the full punishment and condemnation for your sins.
   c. Thank Jesus for His love for you and for His willingness to be executed in your place for all of your sins.
   d. In the name of Jesus, release your offender from their specific offenses that you have not been able to previously forgive.
5. Write down specific behaviors that you can do to express agape-based forgiveness toward your offender (agape love, bless, or pray for). _____.

Chapter 9

THE BIRTH OF
YOUR VISIONS

Where there is no vision, the people perish.
Proverbs 29:18 KJV

Joseph was a true visionary. To experience the magnitude of success he achieved for Potiphar, for the prison warden, and for Pharaoh, he needed a lot more than just interpretations of dreams. In each case, he had to gain a vision for what could be done, followed by a vision to create a plan to get everything done, and then get it all done in record time with record-breaking success. We know this kind of vision, planning, and execution once again flowed out of the wisdom he received through his intimate relationship with God.

As I mentioned in an earlier chapter, I lost six jobs in my first four years after college. During that time my income wasn't even *half* of the average American wage earner. After I got fired from job number six,

Gary Smalley visited me in Phoenix. I told him that no matter how hard I tried, I just couldn't succeed. "I don't understand it," I told him. "I'm not stupid—I have a good IQ. I'm not lazy; I am usually 'first in and last out' at every company I worked for; and I know my craft!" I had a marketing degree, and I understood marketing and consumer behavior.

Joseph Principle #8: Accelerating Achievement with a Vision, a Plan, and a Schedule

---

Gary said, "Let me pray about it."

The next morning he came into the kitchen and asked, "How would you like to be wiser than all your bosses?"

I was twenty-six years old, and my confidence had been decimated. I said, "Yeah, right!"

He said, "No! There's something you could do for two years, and in two years you'll be wiser than all your bosses, and in five years, you'll probably be a millionaire."

As ridiculous as all of that sounded, he had my attention. I said, "Okay, what do I do?"

He said, "There are thirty-one chapters of Proverbs, and there are thirty-one days in the month. Every day, with pencil and paper in hand, read the chapter of Proverbs that corresponds to that day's date. Write down the wisdom and insights you find each day. Do that for two years, which will take you through the book of Proverbs twenty-four times. I promise, it will change everything!"

I started doing exactly what Gary said. Long story short, it *did* change everything!

During the next eighteen months, I went through Proverbs over and over again and found some amazing strategies and incredible insights. I also quickly went through jobs seven and eight, and job number nine lasted only four months. But in those four months, using the strategies I found in Proverbs, I doubled the company's annual sales from $30 million to $60 million. I then decided to quit my job and start a new company with a partner who had $5,000. Six months later, our little company's sales grew from zero to nearly a million dollars *a week*. Everything Gary said would happen did happen, but in about half the time.

A New Insight: Without Versus With

One of the many insights I found in Proverbs was that when a principle is stated in a proverb, the converse of that principle is usually true. Proverbs 29:18 says that *without* a vision, the people *perish*. So, I thought about the converse of that statement, which would be just as true: *with* a vision, the people *live*. And as I looked at Joseph's life, I saw a true man of vision. He not only had dreams, but God inspired him with the vision and wisdom to achieve extraordinary success in everything he did. Any successful entrepreneur will tell you that long before they had success, they gained a specific vision of what they wanted to achieve. And such visions create a passion, and that passion fuels their drive from the beginning until their vision is finally achieved. At the same time, people who don't have a vision of what they want to achieve not only fail to achieve **but also** lose their passion and drive *to* achieve.

> **Without a vision, people, relationships, and projects fade and die, but with a vision, they gain new life and thrive.**

Without a vision, people, relationships, and projects fade and die, but with a vision, they gain new life and thrive.

Joseph had a vision of God and who He really was. He had a vision for his relationship with God. He gained a vision for each project that his master Potiphar assigned to him. Because he achieved so much success on each project, Potiphar put Joseph in charge of everything he owned. He committed his entire estate and all of his business interests to Joseph's management. Later, as we see in Genesis 41, Pharaoh put all of Egypt's affairs under Joseph's charge. Joseph's position and power was second only to Pharaoh. The reason? Pharaoh said, "Since God has made all this known to you, there is no one so discerning and wise as you. You shall be in charge" (Gen. 41:39–40). Once again, Joseph gained a vision for every endeavor he undertook, and then he did everything he needed to do to fulfill each vision.

Visions Critical to Your Life

What are the most important areas of your life? Your relationship with God? Your marriage? Your children? Your work or career? If your relationship with God is important to you, then you need to gain a clear and accurate vision of who God is, what He is like, and what He wants. What does He want to give you, and what does He want in His relationship with you? The same is true for your marriage. You need to gain a clear vision of what you want to see in your marriage, and your spouse needs to do the same. Then, together you can take each other's vision and create a joint vision for your marriage. Gaining a vision in any area of your life or in any relationship will bring new life to that area or relationship. Certainly, the most important visions you will gain are your visions of God the Father, the Son, and the Holy Spirit.

What Is a Vision?

When I speak of a vision, I'm not talking about a dream. I've had only one of those in my lifetime, and it was truly amazing—even miraculous!

But now I'm really talking about two types of visions. One is like a high-definition, crystal-clear photograph, and the other is like a Google map. Gaining a true, accurate vision of God is the high-definition photograph type. God wants us to have that type of vision of Him, the Lord Jesus, and the Holy Spirit. That is what chapter twelve is all about, and it could be the most important chapter in this book.

But right now, we're going to talk about the other kind of vision—the Google Maps type. This is the kind of vision you can gain for any important relationship in your life. You can gain it for any project, endeavor, or pursuit. This type of vision took my sixteen-year-old son from the twentieth-ranked high jumper in the nation to the national champion in one year. It took my thirteen-year-old son from a novice piano player who couldn't read music to performing a solo concert of George Gershwin's *Rhapsody in Blue* in fourteen months. He played the sixteen-minute piece (which was thirty-one pages of music) to a standing-room-only audience of seven hundred. He performed it from memory without a page of music on the piano.

This type of vision allowed me to create more than a thousand television scripts, hundreds of commercials, and dozens of shows, all in ridiculously short periods of time. Those commercials produced more than forty million phone calls and billions of dollars in sales for our start-up company.

How to Gain a Vision

Gaining a vision does not require a mystical experience. Yes, the Holy Spirit may whisper something in your ear or may open your eyes to a need or an opportunity that you've been previously blind to, but oftentimes it's as easy as identifying what you want, what someone else (like your boss or spouse) wants, or what God wants. Take a specific area like your relationship with your spouse or your relationship with God. Ask yourself, "If I could have anything I want in this relationship, what would it be?" Don't limit your question to your own resources, your current situation, or your current limitations. If you had a magic wand and could have *anything* you want in that area, what would it be? Then write that down.

> God wants us to be honest and transparent in our prayers.

Next, pray about it. Remember what we discussed on Philippians 4:6–7 in chapter 4. God wants us to be honest and transparent in our prayers. We hold nothing back but tell Him exactly what we want in a spirit of thankfulness, and then He will give us the supernatural peace to guard our hearts and minds. And when that happens, clarity often comes to our visions. Then, if God wants you to revise your initial vision, write that down.

Google Mapping Your Visions

Imagine you decide you're going to take a two-week driving vacation. Would you ever just load the car with luggage, grab your spouse and kids, and say you're going on a vacation *before* you decide where you're going?

"Come on kids, we're going on a two-week vacation."

"Where are we going?" they'd ask.

You would reply, "I don't know yet, but let's just get in the car and start driving. Sooner or later, we're bound to get someplace where we'll do lots of fun things."

I'm sure your spouse would instantly pull the kids out of the car and tell them to run back into the house. They would then call someone, tell them that you've just lost your mind, and ask them to come to your house immediately.

That, of course, is a scenario so ridiculous you know it would never happen. You wouldn't even think of starting a two-week drive without first mapping out each destination and deciding on the route you would take. You'd decide on the intermediate locations you'd stop at along the way. You would plan how much time you'd spend at each location. You'd plan out the hotels you'd stay at, and you would budget your time and money so you could see and do everything you'd want to see and do throughout the two weeks. You'd certainly talk to your spouse and kids to see what they would want to do during the two weeks as well. Once you had all of that figured out, you'd put your first day's destination into Google Maps, and you'd be ready to start your trip.

Unfortunately, although most people map out their vacations, they do not map out the most important pursuits of their lives. They don't have a map for their marriages, their parenting, their relationship with God, their spiritual pursuits, their careers, or their work projects. They never gain a vision of what they really want. They may have hopes and dreams, but no vision. And without a vision, their hopes, dreams, and pursuits ultimately fade and die.

After I started on job number ten, I began using a process that I originally called *dream conversion*, because it took the dreams in my mind for various projects and converted them into reality. I later called this process *vision mapping*. Solomon wrote, "Do you see a man skillful in his work [diligent in his business]? He will stand before kings" (Prov. 22:29 ESV). This proverb was proven true with Joseph. He might have been one of the most diligent men in history. I'm sure that his amazing diligence, like Solomon's, began with a vision that he then mapped out. In my own life and career I have learned that nothing spawns diligence more than vision mapping. During my television days, our biggest competitor had a marketing department of more than 150 people. We had fewer than five, yet we produced more hits than our top five competitors combined. I vision mapped; they did not. For eight years in a row, we were the most productive company in the United States, generating more sales and profits per employee than any other company, including all of the Fortune 500 companies. That's the power of vision mapping.

The Vision Mapping Process

Vision mapping is not a complicated process. It's simple. But because it takes a little time, most people don't make the effort. Like a raft on a river, they simply "go with the flow" (except when it comes to their vacations). I'm not saying we need to vision map everything or even a lot of things. We only need to vision map the pursuits, endeavors, or projects that are most important to us—the ones in which we really want success. Joseph's interpretations of dreams got him out of prison and into Pharaoh's palace. But they only took him through the front door. His success took him from a prisoner on probation to the second most powerful man in Egypt. His success came from his intimate relationship with God. And the vehicle of his success was the way he could gain visions of what was needed for each endeavor he undertook. I imagine that his visions were crystal clear, enabling him to map out the precise goals and steps to take to diligently pursue everything that needed to be accomplished to turn those visions into tangible realities.

Steps to Creating a Vision Map

1. Get an honest and accurate picture of where you are right now.

Google Maps will not display any route or times without knowing your current location first. The same is true with vision mapping. For example, if you wanted to vision map your relationship with God, you would look at where you are currently in your relationship with Him.

We have more details of David's relationship with God than we have of Joseph's. We can see the health (or lack of it) in his relationship with God at various stages of his life. In assessing where you are right now in your relationship with God, you could ask yourself, "Am I where David was as a young man—a man or woman after God's own heart—passionate in my intimacy and love for Him, where He's more important to me than anything? Am I where David was when he was in the depths of despair after he had committed adultery with the wife of one of his best generals and then had the general murdered?" On a scale of 1 to 10, we could rate young David's passionate intimacy with God as a 9+. After his fall from that intimacy with God, evidenced by the adultery and murder, he would probably score less than a 1 on that same "intimacy with God" scale.

Most likely, you're probably not all the way down to a 1 but probably not a 9+ either. Ask yourself, "Is my prayer life active and productive in drawing my heart closer to a union with His?" How about your active love for those He brings into your path? Your ministry to other believers? Your desire to be a witness for Him both with your life and your words? Where are you right now? If improving your relationship with God is what you would like to vision map, you would write down where you are right now. You would specifically identify the areas of your relationship that you would like to see improved.

2. Determine a clear picture of where you want to go (your desired destination).

Of course, you can't get anywhere with Google Maps until you type in your destination. The same thing is true with vision mapping. For example, you may say that you want a more intimate relationship with God. You want to experience His whispers more often. You want to have a more fulfilling and effective prayer life. You want to experience more of God's amazing agape love, even see His power. You would like to see yourself used by Him to help others become closer to Him.

3. Determine your intermediate stops (goals).

This step is creating the goals that need to be achieved to accomplish your vision. You don't drive nonstop from New York to Los Angeles. You determine your intermediate destinations before you leave your driveway. Same here. To have a more intimate relationship with God, you need to determine the goals you need to achieve in order to create that intimacy. For example:

- Experience a more fulfilling and effective prayer life.
- Get to know more about God.
- Experience His whispers daily.
- Grow your faith.
- Discover God's will in specific areas of your life.
- Be a glove on His hand to do His will and see lives miraculously transformed.
- Become a channel of His love.
- Experience the gifts, ministries, and fruits of the Holy Spirit.

4. Choose the specific routes you need to take to achieve those intermediate goals (steps).

This is defining the steps that you need to take to achieve your first goal. For example, take the first goal: experience a more fulfilling and effective prayer life.

Experience a more fulfilling and effective prayer life (possible steps):

- Discover what Jesus said about praying.
- Discover what Paul said about praying.

- Read other Bible verses on prayer.
- Talk to someone you know who has an amazing prayer life.
- Read a biography of a Christian who was known for their prayer life.

5. Identify the tasks that need to be completed for you to take the identified steps.

Discover what Jesus said about praying:

- Look up "prayer" in *The Greatest Words Ever Spoken*.
- Look up "Jesus' prayers" in *Greatest Words*.
- Google "Jesus' prayers."

6. Assign a completion date for each task and step you want to complete.

Experience a more fulfilling and effective prayer life:

- Discover what Jesus said about praying. (April 19)
  - → Look up "prayer" in *The Greatest Words Ever Spoken*. (April 5)
  - → Look up "Jesus' prayers" in *Greatest Words*. (April 12)
  - → Google "Jesus' prayers." (April 19)

This is the vision mapping process. Simply stated, you identify the vision you want to achieve. Then you determine where you are right now in relation to that vision. Then you create the intermediate goals that need to be accomplished. For each goal, you list the steps that need to be taken, and for each step, you identify the tasks that need to be completed. Finally, you assign a date to each task, step, and goal.

Vision of where you want to be and where you are now
Goals you need to complete to achieve your vision

Steps you need to take to achieve each goal

Tasks you need to complete to take each step

As you can see, creating a vision map is not a complicated process, but it does require a little time. The first time you create a vision map, it may take an hour or two. After you've done it a few times, you'll find it goes a lot faster. Don't think, *Oh no, I don't have an hour or two.* You can do it over a few days or even a week—ten- to fifteen-minute sessions at a time. When you vision map your dreams, you will not only achieve those dreams but achieve them faster than you could have ever imagined. (For another example of the vision mapping process, please see appendix 2.)

> When you vision map your dreams, you will not only achieve those dreams but achieve them faster than you could have ever imagined.

Going back to our example, you may have spent years wanting a more intimate relationship with God but haven't even come close to experiencing it. If you vision map that goal, you are likely to experience it in a few weeks or even in a matter of days. This will also enable you to be more diligent in gaining a vision and achieving it. Look at what Proverbs says about diligent people.

God's Promises to Diligent People

- **You will gain a sure advantage.** "The plans of the diligent lead surely to advantage" (Prov. 21:5 NASB 1995). The advantages you will see with vision mapping are that you will achieve your vision and you'll achieve it in record time.

- **You will experience true fulfillment.** "The soul of the diligent is made fat" (Prov. 13:4 NASB 1995). "The soul" refers to your innermost being. Fulfillment will not be superficial but will reach into the very depths of who you are. That kind of fulfillment is brimming with joy and perseverance.
- **You will gain the respect and admiration of those in authority.** "Do you see a man skilled in his work [diligent in his business]? He will stand before kings" (Prov. 22:29 NASB 1995). Because vision mapping and diligence can result in accomplishing extraordinary outcomes, those outcomes create respect and admiration from others. Once again, we see that clearly in the life of Joseph.

Joseph was a man of many visions, and the accomplishing of those visions in a diligent manner was honored by God and by everyone around him. His intimate relationship with God and the inspiration, vision, and diligence that flowed out of that relationship saved the people of two nations. As you grow in your intimacy with the Lord, you can expect that the inspiration, vision, and diligence that will flow from your relationship with Him will bring blessings, both temporal and eternal, to you and to those whom God brings into your path.

There's no better way to approach vision mapping than to begin the process with prayer. Ask God to help you clarify your vision and ask His help in mapping it out. Ask Him to give you wisdom and to help you find others who could help you in this process. God desires that we gain wisdom (Prov. 4:7) and pursue our most important endeavors with diligence (Prov. 21:5).

Joseph Principle #8: Accelerating Achievement with a Vision, a Plan, and a Schedule

Chapter 10

GOD'S AMAZING CYCLE FOR YOUR VISIONS AND DREAMS

Most assuredly, I say to you, unless a grain of
wheat falls into the ground and dies, it remains
alone; but if it dies, it produces much grain.

John 12:24 NKJV

Birth, Death, and Rebirth of a Vision

Have you ever had a hope, a dream, or a vision for something, only to have it go down in flames? That's happened to me so many times I couldn't count. Every time I started a new job or a new business, I always thought, *This is the one! This is what I'm going to do for the rest of my life!* Yet, nine times in a row, I saw each of those jobs (including two businesses I started) vaporize within a matter of months. My failures in my personal life were even worse. And every time my hopes and dreams died, my heart was brutally crushed. I did not understand the lofty concept of God's sovereignty. When it came to my heartaches and heartbreaks, no belief, no theology, and certainly no doctrine helped in any way at all. Oftentimes, it seemed as if my prayers didn't get past my ceiling, and when I wept, it seemed I was weeping alone.

I imagine that when Joseph was thrown into the well with no food or water, he surely felt the same way. And when his brothers pulled him out of the well, I'm sure his hopes momentarily resurfaced and soared. But within minutes, they were quickly dashed. He was taken to a nearby caravan and sold into slavery. As he saw his brothers turn toward home and walk away without him, he surely experienced a grief beyond anything we can imagine. Remember, he was only seventeen years old. His visions of his brothers and father bowing down to him had certainly filled his mind with dreams and expectations of a future filled with glory and grandeur. Then, in an instant, it was all gone. He knew nothing of the Big Flip that would ultimately change everything.

Joseph Principle #9: Allowing One Vision to Die So a Better Vision May Be Born

How about you? What hopes and dreams have you been so excited about, only to have them crushed, shredded, or vaporized? How did you feel at your time of loss? Did you feel alone? Did you feel that somehow you'd failed? Did you feel that God failed you? How many times have you asked, "Why?" or "What did I do wrong?" or "How could this happen to me?"

What you're going to learn in this chapter is going to give you an understanding of God's amazing love and sovereignty in your life and His purposes for you. You will see that nearly every life story recorded in both the Old and New Testaments reflects the amazing pattern revealed in this ninth Joseph Principle. I first learned this principle at a Bill Gothard seminar when I was twenty-four years old and then saw its power and glory repeated in my life experiences over and over and over again for the next four decades. Bill called it the birth, death, and resurrection or rebirth of a vision. The principle is this: We gain a vision for something— a new relationship, a friendship, a marriage, a relationship with our child, a job, a project, a new pet, a new hobby, a ministry, even our relationship with God. That is the birth of a vision. Then, before the vision becomes fulfilled, it dies. It may be a slow death, or it may be an instant death. When that happens, we lose all hope. After all, it's a death. That is the death of a vision.

This is the point where we have an awesome opportunity to bless and glorify God. We have the chance to trust God and step out in faith. We go off by ourselves and pray about it in secret. We don't tell anyone else how we're praying—it's strictly between us and God. Jesus tells us, "**But when you pray, go into your room, close the door and pray to your Father, who is unseen. Then your Father, who sees what is done in secret, will reward you**" (Matt. 6:6). We thank Him for the death of that vision and express our faith and trust in Him and His love and wisdom. Then, in God's timing, one of three things will happen: (1) God will remove that vision and desire from your life because He's decided it's not in your best interest, (2) God will resurrect your vision and add His blessing to it— making it better than you ever imagined, or (3) He will birth a brand-new vision within your heart and mind and fulfill that newly born vision.

Adam and Eve (Gen. 3)

Birth of a Vision: They have a vision of a wonderful future. They live in a glorious environmental paradise. Their lives and future are full of hope and joy. They get to enjoy wonderful fellowship with God. All God asks of them is that they avoid one no-no.

Death of a Vision: They disobey God, commit sin, and their glorious future dies a terrible death. Their love/trust relationship and fellowship with God is broken, and spiritual darkness and death enters their life experience and the life experiences of all of their future generations.

Rebirth of a New Vision: God promises a Savior who will defeat Satan and provide a means for them and their future generations to inherit eternal life and experience restored intimacy with God.

Abraham (Gen. 17, 22)

Birth of a Vision: He's going to have a son, who will be the progenitor of countless people, and through his seed all mankind will be blessed.

Death of a Vision: God tells him to sacrifice his son, his most beloved and priceless treasure.

Resurrection of a Vision: As he raises his knife to slay his son, the voice of an angel tells Abraham *not* to slay his son, saying, "Do not lay a hand on the boy. . . . Do not do anything to him. Now I know that you fear [revere] God, because you have not withheld from me your son, your only son" (Gen. 22:12). Isaac was spared, Abraham's vision was resurrected with God's blessing, and through his seed, the Savior of the world came forth.

Joseph (Gen. 37, 39–47)

Birth of a Vision: He's chosen by God to be the rising star in his own family. His brothers—even his parents—will bow down to him and honor him above themselves.

Death of a Vision: Ten of his brothers hate him and sell him into a lifetime of slavery in a godless nation.

Rebirth of a New Vision: God remains with him throughout his life, raises him up to be the most successful and honored man in Egypt, and through his actions saves the people of Egypt and Israel from starvation.

Moses (Ex. 2–4)

Birth of a Vision: At forty years of age, he is going to deliver God's people from their generations of enslavement in Egypt and lead them into a promised land of their own.

Death of a Vision: He flees Egypt for his life, taking only the clothes on his back. He spends the next forty years in the desert wilderness.

Resurrection of a Vision: God calls him as a broken, inarticulate eighty-year-old man to deliver the Israelites from their enslavement. He'll do it with his brother and with the miraculous intervention of God. Moses relies on and trusts in the almighty God rather than his own wisdom and charisma to deliver Israel.

Peter (Matt. 16, 26–28; Acts 2)

Birth of a Vision: Jesus is the Christ, the Son of the living God. He will always be with Peter. Peter's strong profession that Jesus is the Christ will be the rock on which Jesus will build His church.

Death of a Vision: Jesus is killed like a murderous criminal. Instead of defending Jesus and being a "rock" of faith, he denied and disavowed Him.

Rebirth of a Vision: The Holy Spirit comes and empowers Peter with courage and agape love, and he fulfills Jesus' commands to feed and lead His sheep and make disciples of all nations by teaching them to obey Jesus' commands.

Saul/Paul (Acts 9, 13)

Birth of a Vision: Saul is going to serve God by pursuing and arresting Jesus' followers, regardless of their age or gender. He will condone the execution of those followers.

Death of a Vision: Jesus stops Saul with a flash of light, causes him to go blind, and tells him to stop his persecution of believers.

Rebirth of a New Vision: Saul becomes fully persuaded that Jesus is the risen Messiah, is given a new name (Paul), and becomes the greatest missionary of all time. He takes the gospel to the Gentiles throughout the known world. His greatest passion becomes knowing Christ (Phil. 3:8).

Examples from My Life

Birth of a Vision: I graduated from high school two years after I gave my life to Christ. I got a letter from the admissions office of a wonderful Bible college, offering me a half scholarship. I was so excited I couldn't see straight. I was going to go to Biola University, become a skilled Bible student, and go into full-time ministry after I graduated. I told my mom and sister (both were believers), and they got excited as well.

Death of a Vision: Then, I told my father. He said, "Absolutely *not*. You're going to go to Arizona State University (ASU) and learn how to make a living. Then, after you graduate, if you still want to go to 'preacher school,' you can." We argued for two weeks. He wouldn't budge. I was devastated. But I had no choice, so I accepted a partial scholarship from ASU.

Rebirth of a Vision: I became involved with Campus Crusade for Christ at ASU and another college. God added His blessing to my ministry, and I had an incredible ministry during my four years of college. I had a chance to lead a lot of college kids to Christ and disciple them. One of these became my best friend in life, and to this day, fifty-two years later, we are still best friends. Thanks, Dad! Even more, thank you, Lord, because You used my atheist dad to bring about Your unimaginable vision and will for my college life.

Birth of a Vision: My sophomore year at ASU, I decided I wanted to organize and manage a Christian singing group that would have a music ministry to colleges all over the state. I formed the group with eight awesome music students. It was a Christian folk group called The New Beginning. During the next year, God really blessed our ministry.

Death of a Vision: Then, the very group I'd started asked me to resign as manager so they could hire a new manager who had promised to heavily promote them and buy the sound equipment they needed. Once again, I was devastated. I had personally recruited each member of the group, and now they were firing me.

Rebirth of a Vision: That night, my roommate's girlfriend saw how depressed I was and asked me what was going on. I told her, and she replied, "Why don't you start a new group?"

I said, "If I did, this time it would be a much larger group, like the Johnny Mann Singers."

She said, "Why don't you announce that you're doing that at our College Life meeting tomorrow night?"

And that's what I did. God added His blessing to the rebirthed vision, and we ended up with a group of seventeen singers and eighteen instruments. Most were music performance majors. The group was awesome, and we had a wonderful ministry during my next two years of college. And because of this, I ended up recruiting Ron Patty to be our director and arranger. He is Sandi Patty's dad and one of the best choral arrangers in the country. Sandi was eleven years old at the time, and she was already amazing us with her talent. Ron and his wife became two of my dearest friends in life and continue to be to this day.

During the fifty-plus years that have followed, I've seen this birth of a vision, death of a vision, rebirth of a vision repeated dozens of times in my personal life, my business life, and my ministry.

Why Is This Principle So Important for Us to Know?

I share this process because, when you understand it, you can avoid deep discouragement and despair when even your most treasured visions die.

You can discover that the death of a vision isn't the final chapter of your happy life. You can be encouraged to turn the next page, and the next, and the next, knowing that God is not finished with you yet. It can bless you tremendously anytime you see your vision and its accompanying hopes vaporized. If God permanently removes your vision, it is in your best interests. Then, when He rebirths a new vision, He will add His blessing to it, and your life will be even more greatly blessed. The death of a vision also gives you a tremendous opportunity to springboard into a more intimate relationship with the Lord, and it gives you an awesome opportunity to trust Him and grow your faith.

> You can discover that the death of a vision isn't the final chapter of your happy life.

Take a few minutes and think back on some of your visions that have died. Did God then give birth to a new vision, or did He give you the original vision back, but with His blessing? Or did He birth a brand-new vision to replace your original one? This would be a good thing for you to journal and record His loving sovereignty.

If your vision died and He never replaced it or blessed a new vision, ask yourself, "Did I continue to trust Him and love Him even through that hard time?" If not, such a loss would be good to treasure hunt.

Learning this principle will not only help you, but you can also teach it to your family and others to help them navigate any current or future losses they experience. During my fifty-seven years of being a believer, every vision that has died has been replaced with a better vision from God. He's never left my cup empty or even half empty. Sooner or later, He has always filled my cup to overflowing. I'm fully persuaded He will do the same for you. This is exactly what David was talking about in Psalm 23. When one of your visions dies, pray Psalm 23, one line at a time. Just know that for the Lord to be your shepherd, you have to be His sheep. And

Jesus said, "**My sheep listen to My voice; I know them, and they follow Me**" (John 10:27 BSB).

Can you think of any of your dreams or visions that have gone through this cycle of birth, death, and rebirth? Can you think of any that are currently in the birth stage? How about the death or rebirth stage? If any are currently in the death stage, I would invite you to pray Psalm 23, one line at a time.

> The LORD is my shepherd,
> I will not be in need.
> He lets me lie down in green pastures;
> He leads me beside quiet waters.
> He restores my soul;
> He guides me in the paths of righteousness
> For the sake of His name.
> Even though I walk through the valley of the shadow of
>   death,
> I fear no evil, for You are with me;
> Your rod and Your staff, they comfort me.
> You prepare a table before me in the presence of my
>   enemies;
> You have anointed my head with oil;
> My cup overflows.
> Certainly goodness and faithfulness will follow me all the
>   days of my life,
> And my dwelling will be in the house of the LORD forever.
>   (NASB)

Joseph Principle #9: Allowing One Vision to Die So a Better Vision May Be Born

Chapter 11

FROM GRIEF TO PEACE TO JOY

> He mourned deeply for his son for a long
> time. His family all tried to comfort him,
> but he refused to be comforted. "I will
> go to my grave mourning for my son," he
> would say, and then he would weep.
>
> *Genesis 37:34–35* NLT

As we can see in the passage above, Jacob was devastated beyond belief when his sons told him that Joseph had been killed. He was truly crushed by the news that his most beloved child had been forever taken from his life. He was mentally and emotionally paralyzed, and his pain was greater than anything he had ever known. There was no medicine he could take, no bandages he could apply that could bring even the slightest relief to his crippling pain. The words and efforts of his family could provide no relief or comfort whatsoever. His grief was so consuming, he didn't even *want* relief. He wanted his son back—and nothing less would suffice. He was living in a nightmare that he couldn't awake from. Jacob loved Joseph so much that he said he would mourn for him every day for the rest of his life.

But Jacob wasn't the only one who suffered a horrible loss. Joseph had lost his mother and father, his brothers, his livelihood, his heritage, his privileges, his entitlements, and his freedom. As a slave in a godless nation, he would have no rights whatsoever. He was guaranteed no future, no medical help, not even life itself, because even a minor infraction could result in his execution. Certainly, Joseph had every reason to grieve and be filled with rage toward his brothers and even toward God. In his mind, he had fully trusted God and had believed in his dreams, yet now he found himself a slave in a foreign land, owned by a complete stranger. Joseph could have fallen into despair, depression, and desperation and could have even attempted suicide.

Joseph Principle #10: Dethroning Grief from God's Throne in Your Heart

Although he likely experienced grief and some of these feelings early on, he certainly didn't linger in them. Instead, we read that he experienced levels of success so startling even his master deduced that God was with Joseph. The truth is that, very early on, Joseph replaced his grief with a trusting relationship with God. Yet Jacob, who had taught Joseph everything he knew about God, could not shed his grief so quickly.

I was once asked, "How is grief different from sorrow?" Sorrow has many causes and may come and go as circumstances change. Grief, on the other hand, usually follows an extraordinary loss—a loss that is often permanent with no relief or resolution in sight.

I have been with several friends shortly after they've learned of the death of one of their children. I can tell you that Jacob's response is the norm, not the exception. Psychologists state that there is no greater level of grief than that which is experienced with the death of a child.[1] In addition to the unrelenting grief, there is often an unimaginable onslaught of remorse and sometimes guilt and shame. It's not uncommon for parents to lose hope of ever getting through their grief, and I've known some who, like Jacob, didn't even want to stop grieving. The premature death of a sibling or a spouse can be similarly devastating and debilitating.

As we start this chapter, you may think, *I don't really want to hear this right now* or *This really doesn't apply to me.* The truth is that sooner or later we *all* deal with grief. Whether we react to it, compartmentalize it, bury it, succumb to it, or simply live with it, grief has an undeniable impact on who we are, how we live, and who we will become in the future. Grief affects us both consciously and subconsciously. It can fill our hearts with guilt, sorrow, anger, and even resentment. Grief can be an obstacle that prevents us from experiencing intimate fellowship with God. It can change who we are and who we can become, and it can terribly change how we deal with others. It can even negatively affect our mental and physical health. Grief can trigger substance abuse, cause depression, and even lead to suicide. It can accelerate aging and the progression of heart disease, neurodegenerative diseases, and autoimmune diseases.[2]

> Grief can be an obstacle that prevents us from experiencing intimate fellowship with God.

That's the bad news. The good news is grief's debilitating grip can be broken, and we can be set free from its devastating consequences. Like quicksand, grief can stop you in your tracks and make the rest of your life miserable, as it did with Jacob, or you can discover what Joseph did and what Jesus' disciples did, and you can use your heartbreak and grief as a springboard into a level of intimacy with God beyond anything you have ever experienced.

A Heart That Loves Deeply Grieves Deeply

Grief is nothing to be ashamed of. God gave us a heart that can freely and greatly love, and the greater our love for someone, the greater our grief, both in intensity and in longevity. Initially, grieving serves a number of very important purposes, both emotionally and physically. However, intense prolonged grief, if not effectively dealt with, can produce all of the negative consequences I've mentioned.

Immediately after a loss, the initial grieving process serves a very important role. First and foremost, it provides a release valve of all of the emotional pressure that's created by a heartbreaking loss. Second, and no less important, it often opens our eyes to the best qualities of the person we are grieving. We often see that our love for that person is greater and deeper than we knew, and we gain a clearer appreciation of the person and their attributes. We come to realize that their good qualities far outweighed their negative ones.

Grieving also makes us more aware of what others go through when they are grieving. You will find yourself being more empathetic, compassionate, and understanding of them. You're also likely to become more patient with them as they grieve. You may even be able to help them through the grieving process in ways that others can't. When the father of my dear friend died, I was directing a television show in California and couldn't make it back to Philadelphia for the funeral. John told me, "Don't worry about it, Steve. I'm going to be so busy and surrounded by my dad's friends, so we wouldn't have any time together anyway."

A few years later, my father died, and John was there. As soon as I saw him, I went over and hugged him and said, "John, I had *no* idea how devastating it was to lose your dad. Now that I know, I am *so* sorry I wasn't there for you."

He answered, "Of course you didn't know—neither did I until I went through it. That's why I'm here, bud! I wanted you to know that I know how much you're hurting, and I just wanted to be here for you." Needless to say, my love for John was instantly multiplied! I also started attending more funerals, realizing what the family members were going through.

Perhaps the greatest single benefit to experiencing a heartbreaking loss (and its accompanying grief) is that they wake you up to realities such as your own mortality, the mortality of your loved ones, and the need to be more proactive in prioritizing your activities to make the best use of your time. Until my father died, I never felt my own mortality. I was forty-six, and for the first time, I truly felt like there was a countdown clock for my life. And I realized it was a countdown clock that would never pause. There would never be a time-out that would stop that clock for even a second. It would just keep counting down until I took my last breath. I have since talked to dozens of other men who said the same thing happened to them when their fathers died.

Dethroning Grief as the Uninvited
Master of Your Life

In 2009 I was asked to bring a twenty-minute devotional for ten thousand women at an Extraordinary Women conference. My son's cancer had been miraculously healed a few months earlier, so I decided to share that experience. When I finished, a woman followed me out of the arena and asked if she could speak with me. I said of course, and she asked me, "What would you have done if your son had *not* been healed?"

I said, "Ma'am, you'd be looking at a very different person. I would be hurting beyond description. Every day I'd have to tell myself to get out of bed. Throughout the day I'd have to tell myself, 'Breathe in and breathe out.' But God would be no less a God of mercy and grace, no less a God of miracles and might. He would just have had a different purpose for my son."

She then told me that, just like my son, her twenty-year-old son had also contracted that same cancer last year. She said, "We prayed and fasted—the whole church prayed and fasted, and even my son prayed and fasted—and he still died." She was crying as she told me the story.

I asked, "Did your son know the Lord?"

She replied, "Yes, he *loved* the Lord!"

"So the problem isn't what happened to him—he fell asleep in his bed and instantly woke up in the glorious presence of the Lord Jesus. And when he woke up, his heart was filled with a level of love, joy, and wonder beyond anything he had ever experienced here on earth."

I then said, "The problem, sweet sister, is with *you*. I believe that you are consumed with grief."

She instantly replied, "I am!"

I said, "You have let grief become the master of your life. You wake up grieving, you grieve throughout the day, and you go to bed grieving. Is that right?" She said yes. I then reminded her that Jesus said, "**No one can serve two masters**" (Matt. 6:24). I said, "You have to make a choice. Do you want grief to be your master, or do you want Jesus to be your master?"

She thought for a second, and then she said of her son, "I just want him to know that I love him." She was doing what most people who lose a child do. She was equating grieving with loving. She felt that if she didn't grieve, it would be the same as not loving him.

I told her, "You loved him his entire life and he knew it. But he's no longer focused on you, your love, or anything else going on here on earth. He is consumed by God's love, and his focus is on Jesus—without any restraints or limitations." I reminded her that Paul said, "Eye has not seen, nor ear heard, nor have entered into the heart of man the things which God has prepared for those who love Him" (1 Cor. 2:9 NKJV). I said, "What your son is experiencing is so amazing that we can't even expand our imagination enough to conceive it. But *you* are still here, and God has a purpose for you and the remainder of your life. When grief steals your heart and mind away from the present moment, your Good Shepherd can't lead you. You can't receive what God wants to give you, and you can't be what He wants you to be."

Making Jesus Your Master Is Not a Once-in-a-Lifetime Decision

She got it! We then prayed together, and she asked Jesus to take back the throne of her heart and mind—and He did! In an instant, her heaviness was relieved, and her eyes sparkled as she rejoiced that Jesus was once again her first love. I told her that this is not a once-in-a-lifetime decision. I said, "Every time you sense that grief is stealing your feelings and thoughts away from the present moment, you need to ask Jesus to take the throne back, and you need to come back into the moment. At first, that may happen fifty times a day—but grief will decrease and Jesus will increase. As time passes, Jesus will rule more of your minutes, hours, and days. You will become more sensitive to the promptings of the Holy Spirit and the whispers of Jesus, and you'll be more sensitive to the needs of those who share the moments with you."

What Specifically Do You Need to Do for Grief to Decrease and Jesus to Increase?

Six months after my father died, I was still experiencing heavy grief. I called Gary Smalley and asked him, "How long will this last? Every time I see an older man with gray hair in a baseball cap, it wipes me out—usually I start crying. How long am I going to be like this?"

Gary didn't even hesitate. He said, "Two years! That's typically how long it takes to move from heavy grief into manageable grief." He then told me the two things that I've already mentioned. He said, "God doesn't want grief to be your master. Jesus still wants to be your Good Shepherd, and He wants you to use this time when your heart is so tender as a springboard for you to get closer to Him than ever. Even while you're deep in grief, He wants to be on the throne of your heart."

> "Even while you're deep in grief, He wants to be on the throne of your heart."

If you are currently grieving any kind of loss, you need to hear the next statement Gary gave me. He said, "God isn't finished with you yet!" I want to say the same thing to you. God isn't finished with you yet! He still has a vital purpose for your every day, and He wants you to follow your Good Shepherd more closely than you ever have before. The question is how we can put grief in its rightful place and keep Jesus in His.

Minutes before Jesus' arrest, He knew His disciples were soon going to experience a level of grief they had never before known. He told them, **"Very truly I tell you, you will weep and mourn while the world rejoices. You will grieve, but your grief will turn to joy. A woman giving birth to a child has pain because her time has come; but when her baby is born she forgets the anguish because of her joy that a child is born into the world. So with you: Now is your time of grief, but I will see you again** and you will rejoice, and no one will take away your joy" (John 16:20–22). Here, Jesus was revealing that the pain and anguish His disciples would experience would be replaced by an unimaginable joy that would be immeasurably greater than the grief they would soon experience. And this joy would be permanent—no one would be able to take it away.

How Can Grief Be Turned into Joy?

The question for us is "How?" How can our grief be turned into an even greater joy, a joy that no one can take away? The answer for us is the same answer Jesus gave His disciples. Jesus said that the one factor that would turn their grief into joy was the fact He would see them again, and at that time, they would rejoice. Why would His appearance after His death turn their grief into a joy that couldn't be taken away by people or circumstances? The answer is obvious: then and only then would they truly believe He was indeed the eternal Son of God. For them, seeing would create their belief.

Shortly before His arrest, Jesus' disciples told Him that they finally believed in Him and His claims. They said, "Now we can see that you know all things and that you do not even need to have anyone ask you questions. This makes us believe that you came from God" (John 16:30).

Jesus quickly challenged their profession when He said, "**Do you now believe? . . . A time is coming and in fact has come when you will be scattered, each to your own home. You will leave me all alone. Yet I am not alone, for my Father is with me**" (vv. 31–32).

They all thought they believed, but the fact was when Jesus was arrested, they all (other than John) forsook Him and ran for their lives, just as He said they would. Whatever belief they had in their minds had not penetrated their hearts. Jesus had to come back from death for their mental beliefs to be transformed into true heart beliefs.

Remember that when Thomas was told by the others that they had seen the resurrected Christ, he replied, "Unless I see the nail marks in his hands and put my finger where the nails were, and put my hand into his side, I will not believe" (John 20:25).

Then, seven days later, came his turning point. Thomas was with the other disciples behind closed doors when Jesus suddenly appeared in the room. Jesus turned to Thomas and said, **"Put your finger here; see my hands. Reach out your hand and put it into my side. Stop doubting and believe"** (v. 27).

Thomas's reply was, "My Lord and My God!" (v. 28). Jesus then made a glorious promise that applies to you and me but didn't apply to those in the room. He promised an even greater blessing to us when He said to Thomas, **"Because you have seen me, you have believed; blessed are those who have not seen and yet have believed"** (v. 29).

Our turning point—where we begin to see our grief transformed into joy—is when our beliefs in Jesus, His resurrection, and His words move from our minds to our hearts. But how are we supposed to see that kind of heart belief become our reality in the middle of a sea of grief? Jesus' command to Thomas in verse 27 is also a command to us. He said, **"Stop doubting and believe."** You see, belief is a choice and an action, not a feeling. We are commanded to believe Him and His words to the point of acting on them. We have something available to us that Thomas did not yet have. We have the recorded words of Jesus.

> Every time we act on His teachings, commands, or promises, our faith grows.

Paul wrote, "Faith comes by hearing, and hearing by the word of Christ" (Rom. 10:17 BSB). We also have the Holy Spirit and His ministry to teach us all things and bring to our memory everything Jesus said (John 14:26). Jesus' words not only grow our faith but also bring His Spirit and His life into our lives (John 6:63). Every time we act on His teachings, commands, or promises, our faith grows. All we need to do is listen to His voice, pray, and do what He says. Although we don't physically see the resurrected Christ, we can experience Him in our spirit.

Once again, Jesus promised heightened blessings to those who haven't seen yet believe. Like you, I have never physically seen Jesus. Yet He's become my best friend. I've experienced His presence for more than five decades. He has never left me, even when I've failed Him terribly. Hundreds of times, His presence has turned my mourning into a joy. As you begin to intentionally bring Jesus' words into your mind, they will flow into your heart, and you will begin to experience His continual presence. Experiencing His living presence in you will break the stranglehold of grief over your heart, mind, attitudes, and activities.

Illusions That Keep People Enslaved to Grief

I don't know anyone who enjoys being submerged in grief. Like I said at the beginning of this chapter, after a loss, grief serves a valuable purpose. But it becomes destructive when it replaces Jesus as the master of our lives. As I've counseled people who have wanted to move from their sea of grief to a safe harbor of peace and joy, I've found that certain attitudes or conscious or subconscious beliefs create obstacles that have been difficult for them to overcome. When we've used Jesus' words to "turn the light on," they have been able to replace the illusions and grief with God's reality and Jesus' amazing joy.

False Belief #1: The event you're grieving and the loss you've experienced happened without God's knowledge or loving care.

It's natural to think that the loss you are grieving happened while God wasn't watching. And if He *was* watching, why didn't He intervene and stop it before it happened? The absolute truth is that whatever loss took place, God was there. But God isn't just focused on this life we are currently in. His perspective is eternal and all encompassing. His love, mercy, righteousness, and justice are not limited by time. Our vision is incredibly limited whereas His has no limits whatsoever. His allowing your loss to take place has an eternal aspect that we cannot see or perceive. Paul wrote, "For I am convinced that neither death nor life, neither angels nor demons, neither the present nor the future, nor any powers, neither height nor depth, nor anything else in all creation, will be able to separate us from the love of God that is in Christ Jesus our Lord" (Rom. 8:38–39). The only question is, will you choose to trust Jesus with this loss, or will you turn your back on Him and choose not to believe Him and His words?

False Belief #2: What was lost was a permanent loss.

Everything we can see and touch is indeed temporary. Everything we can see will pass away from the life we are now living. However, there is an eternal side to life that we cannot see while we are in our temporary state of living here on earth (2 Cor. 4:16–18). We are eternal beings encased in temporary bodies. While our losses may not be recovered in this life, for those who have been born again, every loss will be replaced with that which is infinitely and eternally better and more glorious. We can't even imagine what God has in store for us. Paul wrote, "No eye has seen, no ear has heard, no heart has imagined, what God has prepared for those who love Him" (1 Cor. 2:9 BSB). While we can lose anything that is temporal, we cannot lose anything that is eternal.

False Belief #3: Who we are now and the life we currently live is our permanent condition.

Although we as believers know in our minds that this is not true, we behave as if it is. We act as if this life is *it* and that everyone and everything we embrace and clutch is permanent. We view everything and everyone we lose in this life as a tragedy worth permanently grieving. Nothing could be further from the truth. This is not only an illusion; it's an outright lie. This life and everything in it, as great as it may be, is merely a temporary address with temporary furnishings. God has so much more for us, both now and for eternity. This is why Jesus commanded us not to lay up for ourselves treasures on earth that are simply temporary (Matt. 6:19). Instead, He told us to concentrate on that which is eternal and to set our focus on the eternal things that God values. He said, "**But store up for yourselves treasures in heaven, where moths and vermin do not destroy, and where thieves do not break in and steal**" (v. 20). He went on to say, "**But seek first his kingdom and his righteousness, and all these things will be given to you as well**" (v. 33).

When we continue to grieve a loss, we keep our focus set on the past rather than the present. We not only miss the miracles of the moment but are not able to effectively serve the Lord and His kingdom. Jesus said, "**No one who puts a hand to the plow and looks back is fit for service in the kingdom of God**" (Luke 9:62). The Greek word translated "fit" is the word *euthetos*, which means "useful."[3] This is not a moral condemnation. Rather, it's a matter of pragmatic fact. As I mentioned before, just as a farmer can't plow a straight furrow if he's looking back, we can't effectively serve in God's kingdom when we are looking back.

False Belief #4: This life is better than the life that follows.

As we have already seen, we can't even conceive of the incredible things God has prepared for us. We need to realize God has already proved His unimaginable love for us by sacrificing His own Son so that we could be forgiven and separated from the consequences of

> The God who sacrificed His Son for us will not disappoint us with what He has prepared for us.

our sin. Jesus commanded His disciples and us to take control of our hearts and not let them be stressed or troubled, but instead to trust Him and the Father (John 14:1). The God who sacrificed His Son for us will not disappoint us with what He has prepared for us. If we will trust Him by listening to His Son and do what Jesus tells us, He will replace our temporary losses with eternally permanent gains.

False Belief #5: There's nothing you can do about your grief.

This, too, is an outright lie. There are many things you can do. For example, you can treasure hunt your loss and begin to thank God for the treasures you discover because of your loss. And as we've said throughout this book, Jesus' words are spirit and life. Thoughtfully and prayerfully read and study His words, and they will infuse His Spirit and life into yours.

I recently attended the funeral of my ninety-three-year-old uncle. After he retired from his job at sixty-five, he spent the next twenty-five years serving at his church as a janitor. The world might say, "That's not much of an accomplishment." But in God's economy, he was a "servant of all," which means he was one of the "greatest among you" (Matt. 23:11).

After my grandfather died, my grandmother was bedridden from a stroke for two years. On one of my visits with her she said, "I don't know why God is keeping me alive. I can't do anything. There's no purpose for me to be here. I just want to go home [to heaven] and be with Jim."

I said, "Grandma, you do have a purpose here, or God would take you home! You have eight children, twenty-nine grandchildren, and fifty-eight great-grandchildren, and we all desperately need God's help and guidance every day. *Please* pray for all of us every day. I know God answers your prayers. You can do more for us with your prayers than a billionaire could do for us with his money. So please pray for us."

She lit up, smiled, and said, "I can do that!" I'm 100 percent convinced that her prayers made an incredible impact on my life and the lives of my cousins. The fact is, no matter what we have lost, we can always pray for others and glorify God by thanking Him throughout the day for all of the blessings that remain with us.

False Belief #6: God won't fix things.

This is what Joseph's father, Jacob, thought for a while. He didn't want to be comforted; all he wanted to do was grieve—all day, every day. Believing Joseph was dead, he knew that the one he had loved most in life had been forever taken from him. The truth is God chose not to fix things the way Jacob wanted them fixed. But God did fix things—in a way that would save two nations and greatly glorify Him. Jacob's vision was focused on his small world and his short-term timing. God's vision was infinitely better and bigger than Jacob's. God may not fix things to our liking or in our timing, but He has all eternity to fix things far better and bigger than we can imagine.

By our human standards, Nick Vujicic was born broken beyond repair. He was born with no arms and no legs. At first, his mother refused to hold him or even see him. And when the nurse finally held him in front of her and her husband, they both ran out of the hospital and vomited.

Did God fix Nick? No! Did God do better than fix him? Absolutely! Nick did everything he dreamed of. For example, he learned to swim and ski. But that was just a grain of sand on Nick's beach. Today he's married with four children. He has a worldwide ministry and has authored eight books. *Life Without Limits: Inspiration for a Ridiculously Good Life* has been translated into thirty languages. Most important, he's storing up treasures in heaven by having an impact on millions of people of all ages for God's glory.[4] God *does* fix the unfixable in His way and His timing.

False Belief #7: Your perceived right to keep whoever or whatever you lost was violated.

We all grow up clutching whatever we think we have a right to have. When we lose something or someone we have highly valued, we feel betrayed; we feel like our rights to have that person or that material thing have been violated. We truly feel and act as if we were entitled to that which has been taken from us. Consciously or subconsciously, we feel robbed.

Did you know that it's impossible to feel entitled and be happy at the same time? Feeling entitled creates expectations that are rarely met. And when expectations are not met, we become disappointed and frustrated, and our feelings are hurt. And when these primary emotions are left unresolved, they produce anger, resentment, and ultimately bitterness. But the truth is we aren't entitled to possess anyone or anything. Paul wrote, "You are not your own; you were bought at a price" (1 Cor. 6:19–20). And as you saw in chapter 8, yielding your rights to God creates a miraculous transformation of your heart.

Flee Fantasy and Run to Reality

Many people are quick to say they believe in God and believe in Jesus. But when it comes to a heartbreaking loss such as a death, a divorce, a breakup, a severe injury or illness, or even a financial loss, they behave as if God and Jesus are little more than childhood fantasies. They act as if their tragic loss took place without God caring or even noticing. And when grief overwhelms them, they may overtly or subtly surrender to its ruthless mastery. They act as if God is not sovereign or has turned His back on them. They may still go through the motions—they may pray, read the Bible, and go to church—but they behave as if God is either impotent or uninvolved simply because He didn't prevent the event that created their loss.

Often, the truth is they may have had religion and religious activity but may not have come into a true, intimate relationship with Jesus. Jesus said, "These people honor me with their lips, but their hearts are far from me" (Matt. 15:8). Jesus never called us to merely engage in a religion or religious activity. He called us to enter into a personal and intimate relationship with Him and with God the Father. But because people's relationships with the Lord are often based more on their feelings or faulty notions about God, when a severe trial comes, they may be quickly mastered and enslaved by grief. The fantasy god they have fashioned with their own misconceptions has failed them.

But here's the good news. The real God loves them infinitely more than they know and wants to come into a tangible, real relationship with them through His Son.

Even amid chronic grief you can take Jesus at His word—believe what He says and do as He asks. As we have seen, He is not finished with you yet. No matter how great your loss may be, He still has a purpose for you, a calling for you to fulfill. Don't measure the significance of your calling by worldly standards. Jesus tells us that the "greatest among you" shall be servants of all (Matt. 23:11). The single greatest calling we can have is that which the Father Himself gives to all believers: to spend time to move deeper into intimacy with Him (Jer. 9:24). Jesus tells us how to do that in John 14:21–23.

When grief keeps you from getting to know Jesus more intimately, or keeps you from discovering what He said, or prevents you from living in the present moment, you are letting grief keep you from experiencing intimacy with God. This is a critical fact—it's your intimacy with God that will replace that which you have lost with that which can never be taken away. Paul described it like this: "Therefore we do not lose heart, but though our outer person is decaying, yet our inner person is being renewed day by day. For our momentary, light affliction is producing for us an eternal weight of glory far beyond all comparison, while we look not at the things which are seen, but at the things which are not seen; for the things which are seen are temporal, but the things which are not seen are eternal" (2 Cor. 4:16–18 NASB).

Joseph Principle #10: Dethroning Grief from God's Throne in Your Heart

Chapter 12

GAINING THE VISION OF GOD HE WANTS YOU TO HAVE

No one knows the Father except the Son and
those to whom the Son chooses to reveal him.

Matthew 11:27

When you consider that all Joseph knew about God was what his
father had told him, his faith is even more amazing. He didn't
have any written record, only what had been shared with him. Of course,
we don't know if God gave him a personal revelation. We don't know if
he received any whisperings other than the interpretations God provided.
It's possible that he had nothing, and it's also possible he had personal
encounters with God that were not recorded. Yet his faith in God and his
dependence on Him are obvious from his life. Whatever his knowledge
of God was, it is likely that it was blurry at best.

"Who is God?"

"What is He like?"

"What does He want from me?"

"How can I give God what He wants?"

"What happens if I make Him mad?"

"Can He be happy with me?"

These are questions that nearly everyone has asked, almost from the beginning of time. People have formed their opinions and images of God

Joseph Principle #11: Gaining a True Vision of the True God

based on the opinions of other people, based on the teachings of their religion, and based on their own opinions and inclinations. Because God is referred to as "Father" by Jesus and others, many people have an image of God that reflects their experience with their own fathers. If their father neglected, minimized, or abused them in any way, they may consciously or subconsciously believe those traits to be true of God the Father. If their father was strict or unkind, they may attribute those traits to God the Father. If their father was overly permissive or overly demanding, they may attribute those traits to God.

What have you based your opinions about God on? Unfortunately, according to Jesus, most people's opinions about God are incomplete at best and totally false at worst.

The Absolute Truth

Jesus said, "**No one knows the Father except the Son and those to whom the Son chooses to reveal Him**" (Matt. 11:27). This is not a casual thought expressed by a religious leader. This is an emphatic statement that contains an absolute truth—a truth that, according to Jesus, is not up for debate or subject to any other statements or opinions of anyone else. Jesus came to earth as the only one who knew the Father. He lived with the Father for eternity. He was sent to earth to accomplish the missions the Father had commissioned Him to fulfill. He stated in John 6:46, "**Not that anyone has seen the Father, except the One who is from God; He has seen the Father**" (NASB). Jesus is the only one who has come to earth from the Father and is the only one who can perfectly reveal Him.

> **Jesus is the only one who has come to earth from the Father and is the only one who can perfectly reveal Him.**

You Don't Have to Wait

The great news is that you don't have to wait for Jesus to reveal the Father; He has already revealed Him. He gave His disciples and us more than one hundred statements that tell us precisely who God the Father is, what He wants, and what He doesn't want. He tells us what God thinks of us, what God wants to give us, and what God wants from us. Sadly, most of the believers I am familiar with know very little of what Jesus said about the Father. But without His amazing revelations, a person cannot have an accurate vision of God the Father.

How about you? How familiar are you with the more than one hundred statements Jesus gave His disciples, you, and me about the Father? Remember, only the Son knows the Father, and He has already revealed Him to anyone who will hear His words and receive them. And right now, He's ready to reveal Him to you if you will hear His words and receive them.

Jesus also revealed God perfectly with His life. Jesus' attitudes and actions were such a transparent expression of the Father that Jesus told His disciples, **"He who has seen Me has seen the Father. . . . Believe Me that I am in the Father and the Father in Me"** (John 14:9, 11 NKJV). He explained, **"The words I say to you I do not speak on my own authority. Rather, it is the Father, living in me, who is doing his work"** (John 14:10). Jesus also said, **"I have not spoken on My own, but the Father who sent Me has commanded Me what to say and how to say it"** (John 12:49 BSB). If you want to see how the Father would act in any situation, look at how Jesus acted in such situations. Watch Jesus' actions and hear Him speak with the people and in the situations that are recorded in the four gospels.

"Wait a minute," you say. "That kind of study could take me weeks, even months!" Don't dread it; rejoice in it. Jesus' disciples spent more than three and a half years hanging with Jesus, hearing every word He spoke, watching everything He did, and they couldn't get enough of Him. They always wanted more. When He left them, they were devastated that the One they had come to know and love, the One who answered every important question life could bring, the One who was their doorway to the Father was gone. Had they been given the choice, they would have spent the rest of their lives with Him. I've been meditating on the life and teachings of Jesus almost daily for the past fifteen years, and I still can't get enough of Him.

Do you really want to know God intimately? Then spend the rest of your life by Jesus' side. Become a firsthand witness to His life. Listen intently to everything He says. You will see the Father in Him and hear the Father speak through Him. Make His life and words your primary focus. You'll discover how to use Jesus' words as a springboard into the very deepest level of intimacy with the Father and the Son. Even though Joseph had a foggy vision of God, it was enough for him to fully trust God in every situation, even his very worst of circumstances. Because of the recorded testimonies of Jesus' life and words in the Gospels, you have the opportunity to see the Father and gain a high-definition, crystal-clear vision of Him and His Son.

My dear reader, God really wants you to understand and know Him. He said, "'But let him who glories glory in this, that he understands and [intimately] knows Me, that I am the LORD, exercising lovingkindness, judgment, and righteousness in the earth. For in these I delight,' says the LORD" (Jer. 9:24 NKJV). Here are a few of Jesus' revelations of the Father.

1. God Is Sovereign

Joseph believed this to the point of staking his life on it. When God whispered the interpretation of Pharaoh's dream into his mind's ear, Joseph believed it to the point of acting on it. Since a wrong interpretation would result in Joseph's execution, to even offer an interpretation, Joseph would have to be 100 percent confident in God's sovereignty and the perfect accuracy of His whisper. Joseph was indeed 100 percent confident in both. He believed that God could see the future and sovereignly order the events of the universe. He knew God was always present with him, and he knew God could move the hearts and minds of anyone, even those who didn't believe in Him.

God has not changed. Jesus demonstrated His confidence in God's sovereignty as He stood before Pontius Pilate. Irritated by Jesus' silence, Pilate told Jesus that he had the power to release Him or crucify Him. Jesus showed the Father's sovereignty over men when He told Pilate, "**You would have no power over me if it were not given to you from above**" (John 19:11). Even Pilate was blown away by Jesus' confidence in God.

2. God Loves Us with an Incomparable Love

Jesus declared God's immeasurable love for us in a number of statements. He told us and Nicodemus, "For God so loved the world that he gave his one and only Son, that whoever believes in him shall not perish but have eternal life" (John 3:16). Shortly after I asked Jesus to be my Lord and Savior, a dear friend of mine read the following rendition to a group of us. Its source chose to remain anonymous.

> For God (the greatest lover)
> so loved (the greatest degree)
> the world (the greatest company)
> that He gave (the greatest act)
> His only begotten Son, (the greatest gift)
> that whoever (the greatest offer)
> believes (the greatest simplicity)
> in Him (the greatest attraction)
> shall not perish (the greatest promise)
> but (the greatest difference)
> have (the greatest certainty)
> eternal life. (the greatest possession)

Jesus went on to say, "**For God did not send His Son into the world to condemn the world, but to save the world through Him**" (John 3:17 BSB). I'm sure you can't imagine offering up your child to be tortured and executed for *anyone*, much less for people who couldn't care less about you. Yet that's how great and incomprehensible God's love is for you and me. The apostle Paul wrote, "But God shows his love for us in that while we were still sinners, Christ died for us" (Rom. 5:8 ESV).

3. God Is All-Knowing

Jesus told us that God hears our prayers and answers them. In fact, He said, "**Your Father knows what you need before you ask him**" (Matt. 6:8). He knows us to even the most minute detail. Try to count the number of hairs on your head. You could spend a year trying, but you would never get it right. God not only knows the number of hairs on your head but also knows the number of hairs on everyone's heads (Matt. 10:30).

4. God Is Merciful and Gracious

Jesus said, "Learn what this means: 'I desire mercy, not sacrifice'" (Matt. 9:13). He also said, "He is kind to the ungrateful and wicked. Be merciful, just as your Father is merciful" (Luke 6:35–36). Jesus proclaimed God's grace many times in many ways. For example, He said, "He causes his sun to rise on the evil and the good, and sends rain on the righteous and the unrighteous" (Matt. 5:45).

Often, people think grace and mercy are one and the same, but they are radically different. *Grace* is rightly defined as God's expressing His favor to those who don't deserve it. (That includes all of us.) Everything you and I value in our lives has been given to us by God, not because we did something to deserve His gifts, but because of who He is. He loves us with agape love, not because of who we are or what we have done, but simply because that's who He is.

Grace would be rightly illustrated this way: imagine I come to your church to preach and I say, "Everyone in the first two rows, come up to me after the service, and I'm going to give each of you $500."

You know that three people in the first row told you before the service, "I can't stand Steve Scott; I wish our pastor were preaching today." And in the second row one person told you, "I hate coming to church. I'm only here because my wife makes me come." On the other hand, there's a person in the first row you know is the most Christlike person in the church. You think, *I can't believe he's giving all of them the same five hundred dollars—the ones who don't even believe in God and the ones who love God, the ones who like Steve and the ones who can't stand him.*

That would be a demonstration of me extending grace.

On the other hand, because I don't know any of the people in the first two rows, it would be impossible for me to extend mercy to any of them. Why? Because to extend mercy, there must first be an offense committed by an offender. *Mercy* means extending favor and even forgiveness to an offender who deserves punishment for his or her offensive act or behavior.

Because no one in those first two rows has offended me, there is no need or opportunity to extend mercy.

Conversely, if after the service one of those people comes up to me and punches me in the nose, then I would have everything required to extend mercy. I have an offender, an offense against a victim (me), and the opportunity to justifiably extend punishment or to extend mercy.

All of us have sinned, disobeying God's greatest commands: to love Him with all of our heart, strength, mind, and soul and to love our neighbors to the same degree we love ourselves (Matt. 22:37–39). We have committed countless offenses against our loving, righteous, and merciful God. So, here we stand before a holy God who hates sin and unrighteousness, yet instead of giving us the punishment we deserve, He extends mercy. He sent His perfect, sinless Son to take on Himself all of the wrath and punishment for our sins that we deserve. Our God extended us mercy, and Jesus amazingly obeyed His Father's will to provide the means for us to be forgiven and cleansed from all of our sinful attitudes and behaviors. As Paul said, "God made Him who knew no sin to be sin on our behalf, so that in Him we might become the righteousness of God" (2 Cor. 5:21 BSB).

This is an amazing fact. While we're on this attribute of God's mercy, you might be surprised to learn that if you were to look at the hypothetical gods of mythology and all of the man-conceived gods of all tribes, cultures, and religions, mercy is what separates our God from all other conceived gods. Our God is the only God who delights in exercising mercy to those who offend Him. All gods of man's making delight and even glory in exercising vengeance against those who offend them. Jeremiah 9:24 states, "'But let him who glories glory in this, that he understands and knows Me, that I am the LORD, exercising lovingkindness, judgment, and righteousness in the earth. For in these I delight,' says the LORD" (NKJV). The word that is translated "lovingkindness" here (and "kindness" in other translations) is the Hebrew word *hesed*, which is the same word that is translated as "mercy." We can rightly say that our God delights in exercising mercy. That separates Him from all false gods.

This not only identifies God the Father but reveals Jesus as well. He did the same thing over and over again throughout His life on earth, culminating in sacrificing Himself for us—even praying from the cross, "**Father, forgive them, for they know not what they do**" (Luke 23:34 ESV). Oh, what an amazing Father and Son. Oh, what love. And that agape love flows freely from God to us and into us.

> We can rightly say that our God delights in exercising mercy.

5. God Is Caring, Compassionate, Tenderhearted, and Fair

The fact that God loves us with His agape love means that He exhibits the attributes listed in 1 Corinthians 13. He is patient, kind, doesn't boast, isn't arrogant, doesn't dishonor others, isn't selfish, isn't easily angered, doesn't wave a list of our wrongs in our face, doesn't delight in evil. He rejoices in truth. His love for us never fades or fails. And all of this was proven at Calvary's cross. Jesus said, "**Which of you, if your son asks for bread, will give him a stone? Or if he asks for a fish, will give him a snake? If you, then, though you are evil, know how to give good gifts to your children, how much more will your Father in heaven give good gifts to those who ask him!**" (Matt. 7:9–11).

The truth is that any love or compassion or caring you feel for your children is a mere tiny reflection of God's enormous love for you and everyone else who loves and honors His beloved Son. If you want to see a picture of all this, just look at how Jesus treated children, women, and those who were most looked down on and even despised by society. As we've seen, Jesus said that when we look at Him, when we see His attitudes and behavior, we are seeing the heart and behavior of the Father.

Listed below are a few events from the life of Jesus that reveal the heart and mind of the Father.

When Jesus was asked to teach His disciples how to pray, He gave them an example to follow that we have called the Lord's Prayer. In that prayer He was teaching the disciples to begin with **"Our Father, who is in heaven"** (Matt. 6:9 NASB). This in itself is an amazing revelation—that we mortals could address the very God who created the universe as "our Father." For me, that's so awesome, because I loved and adored my dad. For anyone who had an abusive father, this could be a startling revelation. But regardless of how your father was to you, our Father in heaven is an incredibly loving, merciful, and compassionate Father. During my

A Brief List of Jesus' Interactions That Reveal the Heart and Mind of the Father

With Children	Matthew 19:14
With Women	Luke 8:43
With Samaritans	John 4
With the Sick	Mark 2, John 5, Luke 8, Luke 18
With Sinners	Luke 5, Luke 7
With an Adulterer	John 8
With a Prostitute	Luke 7
With the Rich	Luke 19, Mark 10
With the Poor	Luke 21

nearly sixty years of knowing Him and His Son, I have been continually amazed by His grace and mercy and His love and compassion. I could fill a number of books with stories of His perfectly timed interventions in my life—even when I've turned my back on Him.

For example, in the early 1980s, there was a time when I decided I was done with God. I was driving a convertible with the top down on the

Pacific Coast Highway, about a half mile from my residence. I stopped at a red light, looked up into the sky, and shouted, "God, I don't even believe in You anymore!"

He would have been just and righteous to say, "Steve Scott, I'm done with you," and taken my life right there. But instead He kindly and gently whispered back, "Who are you talking to?"

He had me. I answered, "Okay, I admit You are there, but I'm really, really mad at You."

Did He pull away from me? No, not at all. Over the next few years He demonstrated all of the attributes of agape love that Paul wrote about in 1 Corinthians 13. He gave me hundreds of manifestations of His love, grace, and mercy that were truly undeniable.

> The Father that Jesus reveals in His words and in His life is so amazing our imaginations cannot even begin to comprehend the enormity of His love and mercy.

My dear reader, I just want you to know that the Father that Jesus reveals in His words and in His life is so amazing our imaginations cannot even begin to comprehend the enormity of His love and mercy. Please begin to spend all of the time you can in the Gospels. Through Jesus' words and life events and experiences you can intimately know God to a greater degree than you've ever imagined. And as one of my New Testament professors used to say at the end of every class, "To know Him is to love Him!"

Joseph Principle #11: Gaining a True Vision of the True God

Chapter 13

A GIANT KEY TO JOSEPH'S HAPPINESS IS A GIANT KEY TO YOURS

But the LORD was with Joseph in the prison
and showed him his faithful love.

Genesis 39:21 NLT

A friend of mine was sentenced to prison for violating a securities law. He was released eighteen months later. Shortly after his release he came to speak at a chapel service at our company. He had served his sentence at a minimum-security prison in Pennsylvania where most of the inmates were convicted of white-collar crimes. One of his first comments was, "Even though it's a minimum-security prison, I have to tell you that the moment the cell door closed behind me it hit me: I had been stripped of everything. Everything! My only possessions were the prison uniform I was wearing and the toothbrush they had given me. I had no freedom. I was locked into a cell, and I could leave that cell only when they decided I could. I couldn't see or call my wife and children unless they said I could. When you lose your freedom, you have *nothing*. In reality, I had *no* rights!"

Believe it or not, there are worse things than going to prison, and I'm sure slavery is one of them. I would imagine being a slave in a foreign country is even worse. At least my friend had a prisoner's rights to humane treatment and access to medical care. And even though he said the food was terrible, he was allowed to eat three times a day. A slave has no prisoner's rights—no rights to humane treatment, no rights for legal help, not even a right to eat or sleep. This was the situation in which Joseph found himself at the age of seventeen. He was a foreign slave. He had absolutely no rights at all.

Joseph Principle #12: Yielding Your Perceived Rights to God

Yet he became so successful that he was entrusted with everything his master owned. As we said earlier, his pagan owner could explain his uncanny success in only one way. He rightly deduced that God "was with him" (Gen. 39:3). Later, Joseph was thrown into prison and found himself in even worse circumstances. Once again, no rights whatsoever. But before he knew it, he was in Pharaoh's court. There, as we now know, Joseph was so successful that even a godless pharaoh could think of only one reason anyone could be so successful: God was with him (Gen. 41:37–44).

Joseph's Biggest Disadvantage Became His Greatest Advantage

God wants to be with you in an even better way than He was with Joseph. But before we look at that, let's look at a huge advantage Joseph had over most of us. It wasn't a gift of being able to interpret dreams. His amazing advantage was that he had lost all of his rights. You and I still have our rights. Most of us clutch them tightly, and the moment they're threatened, violated, or taken away, we feel deeply wounded. We believe we have a right to happiness, a right to a good job with good pay and benefits, a right to good health, a right to be listened to, a right to be loved and appreciated, a right to pursue what we want, a right to food we like, a right to housing, a right to have our needs met by our parents, our spouse, our children, our relatives, friends, employers, the government, and on and on. We believe we have so many rights we can't even count them.

The truth is any or all of these perceived rights can be taken away in the blink of an eye—by imprisonment, by war, by quarantines, by friends and loved ones, by employers, and of course by an injury or failing health. When any such right is taken from us, our nature is to react. We protest, rebel, even retreat into despair or depression.

On the other hand, when Joseph's rights were completely taken away from him, he did something very few of us would likely do. Instead of complaining, reacting, or rebelling, he quickly turned to God. He didn't turn to Him in anger. He turned to Him in trust. Joseph had nothing, but he truly believed that God had everything. His faith in God was not a mere feeling or even a religious type of faith but rather a heart-sourced faith that was active, practical, and a "steps of action" faith. As a result, Joseph experienced an intimate relationship with God. God was with him, and it became obvious to anyone and everyone who crossed his path.

> Joseph had nothing, but he truly believed that God had everything.

As a man with no rights, Joseph had no demands and no attitude of entitlement. As a man of no rights, he had no expectations. Everything he received, no matter how small or how great, he received as a valued gift from God—a gift of God's grace and not a well-deserved reward. The apostle Peter wrote, "'God opposes the proud but shows favor to the humble.' Humble yourselves, therefore, under God's mighty hand, that he may lift you up in due time" (1 Pet. 5:5–6). Joseph was humbled to the point of utter humiliation, and then God's mighty hand lifted him to unimaginable heights in His way and in His timing. You see, like moving an empty cup from the shelf to under a water facet, humility put Joseph in the perfect place to receive a continuous flow of God's grace.

Like Joseph, Paul was stripped of his rights and entitlements when he was arrested and thrown into a jail in Philippi. Yet from that jail he wrote an amazing letter to the believers in that city. Even though he sat in a jail cell, bound in chains, Paul wrote, "I know what it is to be in need, and I know what it is to have plenty. I have learned the secret of being content in any and every situation, whether well fed or hungry, whether living in plenty or in want. I can do all this through him who gives me strength" (Phil. 4:12–13). Paul's secret was the same as Joseph's: he learned how to yield his perceived rights to God. He trusted and relied on God for the strength to be content, whether in wealth or abject poverty. His advantage over Joseph was that he was coming to intimately know Jesus. Paul called himself a "prisoner of Christ" (Eph. 3:1 ESV) and a "bondservant of Jesus Christ" (Rom. 1:1 NKJV). We have that same advantage. Like Joseph, we can yield our perceived rights to God. But better than Joseph, we can become a bondservant to our loving, merciful, and compassionate Savior.

"Wait a minute," you say. "I thought I was a child of God." Of course, you are—everyone who has been born again or born of the Spirit is a child of God (John 3). You are also a cherished lamb in the Good Shepherd's flock (John 10). He is also your Savior, and you are one of His saved ones. You are also Jesus' friend if you do what He says (John 15:14). These are all aspects of your multifaceted relationship with God. These are the aspects we quickly claim and embrace, and each one of these aspects bring tremendous blessings. But the aspect that is least known and least embraced by most believers is the very aspect that offers the greatest level of freedom, contentment, happiness, and security. It's the aspect that all of Jesus' disciples joyfully embraced—that of being a bondservant of Christ.

You might ask, "Who on earth wants to become a bondservant?"

Answer: Anyone who wants to be happy and content beyond measure. Anyone who wants to intimately know the loving, compassionate, kind, and merciful Good Shepherd. Anyone who wants to know the ultimate level of security—a security that is more secure than the security of earth, a security that will not only outlive our lives on earth but outlive the earth itself. A security that can never be taken from us by anyone or anything. The bondservant aspect of our relationship with God is not a curse; it's an incredible blessing. It brings the incomparable joy and contentment of yielding our rights to God, knowing that He will take care of us better than we can take care of ourselves. Most important, His security extends to eternity.

What Is a Bondservant and What Does It Mean to Yield My Rights?

In the Hebrew tradition, a bondservant or bondslave was someone who, after being given his or her freedom, made the choice to become a slave to their former master who had freed them or to a new master. If they made that choice, they would be a bondservant to that master for the rest of their life. When we were born again, Jesus freed us from our merciless and unrelenting taskmaster of self-centeredness and sin. Speaking to a crowd in Jerusalem, Jesus said that if they would abide in His words and teachings, they would be His true disciples; they would intimately know the truth, and the truth would set them free (John 8:31–32). (He later identified Himself as *the* Truth!)

Some in the crowd instantly objected and said, "We are Abraham's descendants and have never been slaves of anyone. How can you say that we shall be set free?" (v. 33).

The fact that they would even say this shows how self-deceived they really were. They had been a conquered people for nearly a hundred years. Jesus of course was referring to a whole different kind of enslavement. He instantly replied, **"Very truly I tell you, everyone who sins is a slave to sin"** (v. 34).

With that pronouncement, Jesus was alerting them and us to a little-known fact: sin is a ruthless taskmaster. Instead of enslaving a person from the outside, it enslaves the person from within—taking captive one's innermost being, heart, and soul. Unlike other slave owners that can kill the body but not the soul, sin creates a spiritual cancer that can enslave, infect, incapacitate, and ultimately kill one's very soul. Unless a person is set free from its terrible grip, sin's mortality rate is worse than the worst cancer—100 percent. There is no survival rate.

That's why Paul told us in Ephesians 2 that we were all dead in sin, having no hope (vv. 1, 12). Dead is always 100 percent dead, and no hope means no hope whatsoever. Slaves can be set free by their masters. They can be set free by others who may liberate them. But there is no liberator who can set a person free from their enslavement to sin. There is no doctor or hospital that can cure sin's spiritual cancer as it ravages our souls. That is the hopeless state we were all in before we were born again. In a nutshell, sin takes us captive and at the same time gives us spiritual cancer that kills our spirits.

Then came the one and only Liberator who can set us free. He can not only set us free but can bring us back to life, raising us up from our spiritual death. He's our resurrection and our life-giving, miracle-working Savior. Jesus told the crowd that if they would abide in His word, they would know the truth and the truth would set them free. Seconds later, Jesus identified Himself as the Son (who is the personification of Truth) and said He was the one who would liberate those who were enslaved by sin. He emphatically declared, "**So if the Son sets you free, you will be free indeed**" (John 8:36).

Paul declared, "But because of his great love for us, God, who is rich in mercy, made us alive with Christ even when we were dead in transgressions" (Eph. 2:4–5). God not only brought us back to life from our spiritual death through Jesus, but He liberated us from sin's enslavement, its mastery, its consequences, and its condemnation. Jesus set you and me free from its ruthless control.

Since we have been set free, as a free person we have a choice. We now have the freedom to do what the disciples did: choose to become voluntary bondservants of a new master. Only, this Master isn't ruthless. He doesn't bring captivity or spiritual cancer to our souls. Instead, He delivers agape love, kindness, mercy, protection, and eternal life. Instead of us carrying His burden, He takes our burdens off our shoulders and carries them for us. He is the Good Shepherd who loves His sheep and gives them eternal life.

> He is the Good Shepherd who loves His sheep and gives them eternal life.

Along with the Father, He protects us from all others by keeping us safe in His and the Father's hands (John 10:27–29). That's why Peter could tell us, "[Cast] all your care upon Him, for He cares for you" (1 Pet. 5:7 NKJV).

Yielding Your Rights to the God Who Loves You More than You Love Yourself

Unlike the ancient Hebrew tradition, becoming a bondservant of Christ is not a onetime decision. It's a decision that we make every day and sometimes numerous times throughout the day. Since the Son freed you from your previous master, you are now "free indeed" to choose Him to be your new master, moment-by-moment, decision by decision. We do this by yielding our rights throughout the day, and as Paul wrote, we capture every thought and decision and bring it captive into our obedience to Christ (2 Cor. 10:5). Do we do it perfectly? Of course not. But we choose this direction rather than turning our backs on Christ and resurrendering to the enslavement of our old master.

I first met Gary Smalley, the man who introduced me to the first Joseph Principle—and the man who would become my best friend and mentor—in February of 1974. He was speaking to a group of two hundred leaders, preparing us for an upcoming seminar. That night was truly a turning point in my life. Gary's talk was on Philippians 2:5–11. In this passage Paul said that we must have the same attitude as Christ, who had all of the rights that God had but emptied Himself of all of His rights, took the form of a bondservant (to His Father), and agreed to be born in the likeness of men. Jesus then humbled Himself by becoming obedient to the point of death, even death on the cross. And because of this, God the Father exalted Him to the highest position of honor, that at the mere mention of His name, one day the knee of everyone on the earth, below the earth, and above the earth would bow and every tongue would proclaim Jesus as Lord.

According to Gary, Paul was declaring that we should be willing to let go of our perceived rights the same way that Jesus let go of His actual rights. Our rights are only perceived; they aren't real. We act as if they are real, but they are not. As I mentioned earlier, numerous events can instantly steal our rights away. If they can be easily stolen from us, they really aren't permanent rights at all. They are truly only perceived rights.

Yet our efforts to hold on to those rights don't make us happy or secure at all. In fact, they do just the opposite. Trying to hold on to them creates insecurity, anxiety, fear, stress, and paranoia. And when they are threatened or lost, we feel victimized and become angry, bitter, and resentful toward the person who offended or victimized us.

Equally bad, holding on to them and our desire to increase our rights create an attitude of entitlement. An attitude of entitlement makes gratefulness and true happiness impossible to experience. Gratefulness is the only fertile soil in which happiness can take root and grow. If you want to cling to your perceived rights and feed your attitude of entitlement, go ahead. But you'll never know security, contentment, or the peace and joy that only Jesus can give.

On the other hand, if you yield your rights like Jesus, like Joseph, like Paul and Peter and the other disciples, you will gain the peace, joy, contentment, and security that only Jesus can give.

Understanding Our Perceived Rights—FROMPTH

This raises two questions: (1) What perceived rights do we hold on to? and (2) How do we yield them to God? We are so accustomed to holding on to our rights that they are nearly invisible to us. In fact, they are often buried in our subconscious, so we don't even think about them. Yet they may dictate our attitudes and behaviors. But Gary gave me a foolproof detection system that I'll share with you. He said that usually when we become angry, it's because one or more of our perceived rights have been violated or threatened. Anytime we feel hurt or frustrated by the attitudes or behavior of someone else, it's usually because they have violated our perceived rights.

Gary believed that all of our perceived rights could be categorized into seven categories. He created the acronym FROMPTH to remind him of those categories. There's nothing inherently wrong with any of these categories, but a conscious or subconscious belief that we have a claim to those perceived rights and clinging to them interferes with our loving others and God with agape love. It interferes with us living as loving bondservants of Jesus. Here are the seven categories of our perceived rights.

F: Future

We wrongly perceive that we have a right to our circumstances remaining the same or getting better in the future. We feel entitled to a better future and raise our expectations accordingly. Then, when our expectations aren't met, we experience all the negative emotions that accompany unmet expectations. Of course, there's nothing wrong with wanting a better future, but viewing a better future as a right or an entitlement sets us up for disappointment, discouragement, depression, anger, resentment, and bitterness. Yielding our rights to a better future removes our expectations and entitlement mentality and creates an opportunity for gratefulness to grow and happiness to increase.

R: Respect

We all believe we have a right to be respected by others and have a good reputation. Our perceived right to be respected becomes an expectation and can evolve into something we truly believe we are entitled to. In fact, we may demand it. When we don't get the respect that we believe we're entitled to, we begin a downward cycle through all of the negative emotions of feeling like a victim. This can be devastating to a relationship. While everyone wants to be respected, the number one need of a man is to feel admired and respected. Any relationship that doesn't provide that respect will result in the man pulling away from that relationship emotionally and often physically.

O: Others

We have a perceived right to fulfilling relationships with others. We all want other people to like us and even meet our perceived needs. We are more focused on others meeting our needs than we are focused on meeting their needs. We perceive that we have a right to be loved, honored, and served by others. When they fail to meet those perceived needs, we become hurt and frustrated and feel insecure in the relationship. Those unresolved negative feelings create anger, resentment, and bitterness.

M: Money

No matter how much money we have, no matter how much we get, it seems we always want more. It's one thing to *want* more, but believing we have a *right* to more is a right that we simply don't have. But when someone or something takes our money from us or prevents us from gaining the income we feel we have a right to, we become defensive and even take the offensive to retaliate against the offender. Once again, the desire to make money and keep money is not inherently wrong. It's believing and acting as if we have a right to it that sets our feet in spiritual quicksand.

P: Possessions

We perceive that we have a right to possessions. A house, a nicer house, a nicer car, nicer clothes, a nicer TV, season tickets to our favorite sports team, and on and on. People all around us have more and better things than we do and we think, *Hey, I'm a child of God, a "King's Kid." Why shouldn't I have everything they have and more?* Perceiving that we have such rights not only interferes with our relationship with God but can give birth to envy and coveting what others have that we don't have. Worst of all, it can divert our hearts away from God. We literally begin to love and treasure things more than we treasure God and others. These things steal our time and focus away from all that is of eternal worth.

That's why Jesus gave us this love-based warning: "**Do not store up for yourselves treasures on earth, where moths and vermin destroy, and where thieves break in and steal. But store up for yourselves treasures in heaven, where moths and vermin do not destroy, and where thieves do not break in and steal. For where your treasure is, there your heart will be also**" (Matt. 6:19–21).

Jesus sees our pursuit of things as a path that can not only turn our hearts away from God and everything of eternal worth but can plunge us over a deadly spiritual cliff. Thinking and behaving like we have a right to bigger and better creates a poison that will not only make our souls sick but be spiritually fatal.

T: Time

How often have you been asked or told to do something and you felt that request or demand is an infringement on your time? Maybe you've thought, *It's my time, and I'll spend it any way I want. Ugh.* No, if we are a bondservant of Christ, it's *His* time, and we should spend it the way He wants. When we spend our time doing and being what He wants, we are storing up eternal treasures in heaven.

Jesus had the right to spend an uninterrupted eternity with the Father. But He emptied Himself of that right and humbled Himself to become a baby in a manger and a man on a cross. He gave up His right to His time so that He could love the Father the way the Father wants to be loved and could use His time to serve the Father and save you and me. If we are followers of Christ, then as our Good Shepherd, our time belongs to Him. He will lead us, feed us, protect us, and guide us on the right paths on earth and all the way to heaven. He wants us to be good and responsible stewards of our time. It's our most precious commodity, and it's the only one that can never be reclaimed or recovered once spent.

H: Health

Finally, we believe we have a right to good health. Once again, there's nothing wrong with wanting to be healthy. We should do everything we can to maintain good health. But we don't have a right to it. And if we think we do, whenever it's diminished by injury, disease, or the aging process, we will become discouraged, depressed, angry, and very likely bitter.

For more than twenty years, Elmer Lappen was the campus director of Campus Crusade for Christ at Arizona State University. As a student, he had been a track star. But early in his life he contracted rheumatoid arthritis. By the time I met him he was in a wheelchair. Every joint in his body was ravaged by this merciless disease. When any joint moved, you would hear it crackling and you would see Elmer wince in pain. The only joints in his body that weren't affected were those in his jaw. For more than twenty years he preached and taught and sang. I was one of thousands of students whose lives were radically affected by this selfless, godly man. He was truly a bondservant of Christ. When he died, more than ten thousand people showed up at his memorial service at ASU's football stadium.

Of course, Elmer would have preferred to have a body that was free of disease and pain. But thank God he never felt he had a right to it. He would have been a completely different man and certainly would not have had the impact for Christ that he had on me and many thousands of others. I know of many believers who, after losing their health or the partial or full use of their bodies, have had extraordinary ministries in the lives of thousands of others. Some have had an impact on *millions* for the cause of Christ. Had they clung to their perceived rights to a healthy body, they would have been completely different people, and the blessings they have provided to so many would never have been given or received.

The How-Tos of Yielding Your Rights to God   DDACT

Yielding our rights is something we need to do every day and often several times a day. This is what Jesus was referring to when He told us, "**If anyone desires to come after Me, let him deny himself, and take up his cross daily, and follow Me**" (Luke 9:23 NKJV). Denying yourself and taking up your cross daily is not self-abasement. It's simply yielding your rights to God whenever there's a choice between His will and yours. Here again we have an acronym, DDACT: Detect, Determine, Ask, Choose, Thank.

D: Detect

The first step in yielding our rights is detection—detecting the right or rights you need to yield at any given moment. Just as there are red flags that signal us that our mind is in the future or past and not in the moment, there are red flags signaling when we have dropped our cross and picked up our rights. For example, hurt, frustration, anxiety, fear, irritation, and anger are red flags that can reveal we are clinging to our perceived rights in whatever situation that is creating those negative feelings.

D: Determine

The next step is to determine which specific areas of rights are being held on to. For example, maybe you heard that a friend has said something mean about you. Your natural response is to feel hurt. The hurt quickly turns into anger and resentment. You think of FROMPTH and ask yourself, "Which of those seven perceived rights has been violated? Future, Respect, Others, Money, Possessions, Time, or Health?" In this case you may decide your right to be respected and your right to be valued by others have been trounced on.

A: Ask

You ask Jesus or the Holy Spirit to whisper Jesus' applicable words or teachings to you. Instantly you hear His words in your mind like, "**Blessed are you when people insult you, persecute you and falsely say all kinds of evil against you because of me. Rejoice and be glad, because great is your reward in heaven, for in the same way they persecuted the prophets** who were before you" (Matt. 5:11–12). Or He might whisper, "**Love your enemies, do good to those who hate you, bless those who curse you, pray for those who mistreat you**" (Luke 6:27–28).

C: Choose

Then you have a simple choice—the fork in the road. Do you choose to clutch your rights to be respected and valued by others, or do you choose to lay down your rights and pick up your cross and do what Jesus said: rejoice, be glad, pray a blessing on that person, or bless them in some other tangible way and pray for them? You think, *Wow, if I do what Jesus said, I am loving the Father and Son with Their love language and consequently can expect more intimacy with the Father and Son.* You realize that this person's gossip and slander are now springboards into more intimacy with God and more rewards in heaven. Their attempt to damage your reputation has actually turned into a blessing with eternal fruit. You thank God for that person and their attempt to hurt you, and because you're doing what Jesus said, you're bearing "much fruit" and bringing glory to the Father (John 15:6–8).

T: Thank

You thank God for this trial and all the blessings it offers you!

Another example: you get fired from your job. (I had lots of experience with this one.) Here's how you might follow DDACT to move forward in a God-honoring way:

1. **Detect.** Red flags include feelings of humiliation, embarrassment, hurt, anger, discouragement, fear, and despair.
2. **Determine.** Which of your perceived rights was violated? Remember FROMPTH. This one event has violated your perceived rights in all seven of the categories.

→ F—your future is now headed for change.

→ R—your right to be respected and maintain a good reputation has been violated.

→ O—Your boss has treated you despicably, and you're humiliated in front of your peers.

→ M—Your money has just been reduced and 100 percent of your income is gone.

→ P—You may be losing your home and other possessions if you can't find another job fast enough.

→ T—Your planned use of your time has just been detoured—no vacation because you lost your job and you're going to have to divert your time to hunting for a new job.

→ H—Your health and resistance may take a downturn because you're heavily stressed.

Wow, one action violated every category of your perceived rights!

3. **Ask.** Once you ask Jesus or the Holy Spirit to whisper His words into your mind, He might answer with one of the following:

→ He might whisper, "**In this world you will have trouble. But take heart! I have overcome the world**" (John 16:33).

→ He might whisper, "**Ask and it will be given to you; seek and you will find; knock and the door will be opened to you. For everyone who asks receives; the one who seeks finds; and to the one who knocks, the door will be opened**" (Matt. 7:7–8).

→ He might whisper a passage of Scripture for you to meditate on. He might even whisper what you should do next.

→ If you're angry, be transparent and pray according to Philippians 4:6–7. He might whisper, "Forgive them and pray for them and pronounce a blessing on them and their families."

→ He might whisper, "**Come to me, all you who are weary and burdened, and I will give you rest. Take my yoke upon you and learn from me, for I am gentle and humble in heart, and you will find rest for your souls. For my yoke is easy and my burden is light**" (Matt. 11:28–30).

→ If He doesn't whisper anything right away, read the Gospel of John or the Sermon on the Mount (Matt. 5–7).

→ He might tell you to read Psalm 23 or the Beatitudes.

→ He might even tell you to call a pastor, a friend, or someone you can pour your heart out to.

4. **Choose.** Now that you know that your rights have been violated, you're once again at the fork in the road. You have a choice. Cling to your rights and experience all of the negative consequences, or yield your rights and pick up your cross and do what Jesus says.

5. **Thank.** Go off alone and pray in secret and thank God for this opportunity to springboard into greater intimacy with Him and for the opportunity to trust Him in this situation.

As you learn to follow this simple routine to yield your rights, you will find peace, joy, contentment, and security that no one in the world can take away from you. Speaking of you, your Good Shepherd said, "**My sheep listen to my voice; I know them, and they follow me. I give them eternal life, and they shall never perish; no one will snatch them out of my hand. My Father, who has given them to me, is greater than all; no one can snatch them out of my Father's hand. I and the Father are one**" (John 10:27–30).

And now we turn the spotlight toward you. Can you think of any conflict you are currently experiencing where you have been clinging to your rights? Usually, all you have to do is think about the last time someone hurt your feelings or made you angry. Why not grab a journal or notebook and use this DDACT process to discover which of your rights were violated? Then choose to yield those rights to God and enter into the glorious place of His peace and joy—a special place that is a spiritual oasis for those who choose to serve as a bondservant of Jesus.

Joseph Principle #12: Yielding Your Perceived Rights to God

CONCLUSION

Jesus Reveals God's Personal Desires

This is My beloved Son, in whom I
am well pleased. Listen to Him!
Matthew 17:5 BSB

The Two Most Important Questions
You Will Ever Ask

The two most important questions any believer can ever ask are (1) What does God , n want from me? and (2) How can I give Him what He wants? We've already seen from Jeremiah 9:23–24 that God wants us to understand and intimately know Him. We have learned that we come into that intimacy by using His and Jesus' love language of hearing and doing what Jesus commanded and taught (John 14:21–24). Jesus also revealed a number of the Father's other desires. Amazingly, the Father's desires don't weigh us down; they produce tremendous blessings for us and for those whom we influence and interact with. He wants to bless us with a Mount Everest of blessings that affect us not only during our current life but for eternity as well. I've taken the time to create a very small, partial list of God's desires that Jesus revealed in His words. Even though some of this is repetitive of what we have seen in previous chapters, I felt that this list would be woefully inadequate if I didn't include each of these callouts of Jesus' revelations of the Father's desires.

God's Desires for His Relationship with You

1. God the Father Is on Your Side

We've already talked about God's amazing love for us throughout this book. Yet I believe that so many of us often think God is a policeman (an arresting officer), a tough judge, a prosecutor, and an unsympathetic jury. We may think, *Sure, He's on everyone else's side, but I'm not sure He's on mine.* The first thing Jesus alerts us to is that God's love for us is not only a greater love than we have ever experienced, but it is a radically different type of love. Its attributes cannot be manufactured by our human nature. Could our love for our personal enemies ever be so great that we would send our only child into the enemy's territory to purposely allow him to be tortured and crucified to save the very people who mock, torture, and kill him? That is a love that goes beyond anything we can imagine. That is the love that the Father has for you and me. Our Good Shepherd, the Lord Jesus, loves us with that same intense love as well. Jesus said, "**Even as the Son of Man came not to be served but to serve, and to give his life as a ransom for many**" (Matt. 20:28 ESV).

2. The Father Wants to Be Worshipped in Spirit and in Truth

Jesus told the woman at the well, "**But the hour is coming, and now is, when the true worshipers will worship the Father in spirit and truth; for the Father is seeking such to worship Him. God is Spirit, and those who worship Him must worship in spirit and truth**" (John 4:23–24 NKJV). From this passage, it's obvious that if we want to worship God, we need to worship Him not just with our mouths but with our spirits as well. But here, Jesus tells us that we must also worship God in truth. To worship God in truth, we must first know the truth about Him—who He truly is, what He is like, and what He values and doesn't value. Second, we must be truthful in our worship and relationship with God. This is where the prayer diamond of Philippians 4:6–7 comes in. We don't have to pretend to be someone or something we are not. He wants us to be honest and transparent in our prayers and in all of our fellowship with Him.

3. The Father Doesn't Judge Anyone

In John 5:22, Jesus said, "**Moreover, the Father judges no one, but has entrusted all judgment to the Son.**" Jesus went on to say that the Father turned all judgment over to the Son, because Jesus became the Son of Man. Thus, the Father wanted to honor Jesus, and He wants all of humanity to honor His beloved Son. This is so important to the Father that Jesus said anyone who does not honor the Son does not honor the Father (John 5:23). Thus, Jesus not only has the perfect moral ability to righteously judge everyone, but the Father has also transferred to Jesus all the authority to judge.

Yet Jesus tells us that even though He has the ability to perfectly judge us, and even though the Father has given Him all of the authority to do so, He still doesn't judge anyone (John 8:15). He said, "**For I did not come to judge the world, but to save the world**" (John 12:47). However, Jesus went on to say, "**There is a judge for the one who rejects Me and does not receive My words: The word that I have spoken will judge him on the last day**" (John 12:48 BSB). Jesus told Nicodemus, "**For God did not send his Son into the world to condemn the world, but to save the world through him**" (John 3:17). This helps us to understand why it's so offensive to God when we judge others. Both the Father and the Son have the ability and the authority to perfectly judge others, yet They choose not to judge. They leave that judgment and the standards of judgment to the perfect spoken words of Jesus, and those words provide the standard by which people who reject Jesus and His words will be judged.

4. The Father Wants Us to Hear and Do What Jesus Says

As we saw in chapter 5, at the transfiguration, God was crystal clear in His instructions to Peter, James, and John. "This is my Son, whom I love; with him I am well pleased. Listen to Him!" We also saw in chapter 6 that Jesus connects His and the Father's love to our hearing and doing what Jesus said. He gives us the promise of His and the Father's continual presence and intimacy if we will simply hear Jesus' commands and teachings and obey them. We don't need to ask the question, "What would Jesus do?" because in most cases there's no way we can answer that question with clarity and certainty. However, in any situation we encounter we *can* ask, "What did Jesus say?" and what Jesus said is crystal clear. For those who meditate on His words, the Holy Spirit will perform His ministry and remind us of what Jesus said (John 14:26).

5. The Father Wants to Give the Holy Spirit and Other Incredible Gifts to You

Throughout my life as a believer, there were many times I found myself pleading to the Father for something I felt I desperately needed. In a desperate situation, this is our natural response. But Jesus turns the light on when He tells us that the Father's nature is to love and to give. He is not a stingy God. He loves to give good gifts to those who follow His Son. In fact, Jesus tells us that the joy and gratification we experience when we give gifts to our children is a tiny sample of God's desire to give us good gifts. He said, "**If you, then, though you are evil, know how to give good gifts to your children, how much more will your Father in heaven give good gifts to those who ask him!**" (Matt. 7:11). We don't have to plead or beg; we simply need to ask.

However, remember that His priorities always have our eternal best in mind. Those unanswered prayers that we've all experienced at times are not unanswered prayers at all. In those cases, a no or a "Not now" is God answering us according to what's best for us, for others, and for His kingdom in relation to eternity. Jesus' three prayers to be spared the agony of bearing our sins were answered. But they weren't answered in a way that would have met Jesus' temporary need; rather, they were answered in a way that would glorify Jesus for eternity, fulfill the Father's will for redeeming us, and benefit all of Jesus' followers then, now, and for eternity. We often look at what's right in front of us and think that is what life is about. But Jesus told us that the Father wants us to seek first His kingdom. Paul said it perfectly when he wrote, "Therefore we do not lose heart. Though outwardly we are wasting away, yet inwardly we are being renewed day by day. For our light and momentary troubles are achieving for us an eternal glory that far outweighs them all. So we fix our eyes not on what is seen, but on what is unseen, since what is seen is temporary, but what is unseen is eternal" (2 Cor. 4:16–18).

The Father wants us to be ever mindful that this earth is not our home—it's just a temporary residence. He wants us to realize that everything we can see and touch right now is only temporary, but we are eternal. He will always act with our eternal best as His priority. God knows that our greatest need in this life is for the indwelling presence of the Holy Spirit and the ministries, the power, and the fruit of the Holy Spirit. Here again, He isn't stingy. He doesn't withhold the Holy Spirit from us until we become "worthy" to receive Him. Rather, He delights in sending the Holy Spirit to minister to us and through us. Jesus tells us, "**If you then, though you are evil, know how to give good gifts to your children, how much more will your Father in heaven give the Holy Spirit to those who ask him!**" (Luke 11:13).

6. The Father Wants You to Trust in His Loving Sovereignty and Protection and Follow Your Good Shepherd

Joseph's foundational belief, which everything in his life was built on, was that God was sovereign in all things and that He loved Joseph. That belief produced immovable faith that could not be shaken, even by the terrible circumstances that engulfed him. The Father wants us to embrace those same beliefs. Jesus said, "**My sheep listen to my voice; I know them, and they follow me. I give them eternal life, and they shall never perish; no one will snatch them out of my hand. My Father, who has given them to me, is greater than all; no one can snatch them out of my Father's hand**" (John 10:27–29). How secure should we feel, knowing that we are safe in the hands of the Father and the Good Shepherd?

7. The Father Wants You to Forgive

As we saw in chapter 8, the Father wants us to forgive because He has forgiven us. Unforgiveness sends a loud and clear message to the Father that we are not grateful for His forgiveness. We have a casual appreciation of the sacrifice He and His only begotten Son made, but not so much that we will follow His command or example.

On the other hand, to forgive is showing the Father that we are grateful for His grace and mercy and are truly following our Good Shepherd, who prayed, "**Father, forgive them, for they know not what they do**" (Luke 23:34 ESV). God forgives us not because we deserve it but because of who He is. We forgive others not because they deserve it but because of who Jesus is and because of what He's done for us.

8. The Father Wants You to Abide in Jesus' Words So You Can Bear Much Fruit

God has a purpose for keeping you alive here on earth. His purposes for you are both temporal and eternal. His purposes include those that are just for you and for your growth in your intimacy with Him as well as for your interaction and influence with others. At the Last Supper, Jesus gave His disciples and us a picture of a vine, its branches, and the fruit that grows on the branches. He told us that He is the vine and the Father is the gardener. He then told us that we are the branches. Everyone knows that the vine isn't placed into a garden merely for its looks. Rather, its sole purpose is to produce fruit—fruit that benefits the gardener. The fruit will also benefit anyone the gardener chooses to share it with. Jesus said if the branch doesn't produce fruit, it's cut off and thrown into the fire. If it does produce fruit, the gardener lovingly prunes or trims it so it can produce even more fruit (John 15:1–8).

Jesus gives us this analogy to emphasize that we are not here just for ourselves. He then makes two critical points. First, without Him, we can do nothing. All of our eternal worth and our ability to produce eternal blessings for others is entirely dependent on remaining connected to Him. It's impossible for any branch of any vine to produce fruit if it is separated from the vine. If we are separated from our vine (Jesus), it's just as impossible for us to produce any fruit that is pleasing to God or eternally beneficial to others. Jesus said, **"Apart from Me you can do nothing"** (John 15:5 NASB).

Then in verses 7 and 8 comes the big reveal. In these two verses, Jesus showed us how to produce a lot of fruit, how to have our prayers answered with yeses instead of noes, and how we as finite human beings can bring glory to our Father, the eternal and infinite God. Jesus said, **"If you abide in Me, and My words abide in you, you will ask what you desire, and it shall be done for you. By this My Father is glorified, that you bear much fruit; so you will be My disciples"** (NKJV). This is a conditional promise. If we meet only two conditions, three extraordinary benefits are promised.

- Condition One: If we abide in Jesus.
- Condition Two: If His words abide in us.

- Promised Benefit One: God will give us the desires we pray for.
- Promised Benefit Two: We will bear much fruit.
- Promised Benefit Three: We will glorify God.

The Greek verb *meno* is translated as "abide." It means to come to a stop and remain in a particular place. Picture that you were walking from your house to a place ten miles away. But after walking five miles you decide to stop, sit down for twenty minutes, and remain there to rest and have a drink of water. For those twenty minutes, you would be abiding in that place.

If you abide in a tent or a building, the noun derivative of *meno* is *mone*. *Mone* means "a place to reside or dwell" and is usually translated as the English word *abode*. Jesus is telling us that if, in our journey through our hours, days, weeks, and months, we will let our hearts and minds reside in Him and His words, and if we will let His words reside in our minds and hearts, then we will be fulfilling the two conditions of abiding in Him and letting His words abide in us. Reading and thinking about Jesus' words in the Gospels will help us to abide in Him and will enable His words to take up residence in our minds and hearts. As we do this, the three promised benefits of John 15:7–8 will be given to us. Our desires will morph into a reflection of the Father's will. As we then pray for those desires, God will wonderfully answer our prayers with His yeses. The end result will be that we will bear much fruit, and God the Father will be glorified by us and by the fruit we bear.

Bearing fruit involves two aspects. The first is becoming an open channel for the Holy Spirit to produce in us His fruit—the fruit of the Spirit. The fruit of the Spirit is agape love, joy, peace, patience, kindness, goodness, faithfulness, gentleness, and self-control (Gal. 5:22–23).

Amazing! We receive more love, joy, peace, patience, goodness, faithfulness, gentleness, and self-control, and God receives more glory. God will use this fruit to grow our faith and bring more joy, peace, and contentment into our lives. That fruit will increase our intimate fellowship with the Lord and bless the lives of others.

This is what Jesus was referring to when He said, "**Whoever believes in me, as Scripture has said, rivers of living water will flow from within them**" (John 7:38). These rivers of living water that flow from the Holy Spirit within us not only give us the life we desperately desire but also give life to those who cross our paths. Jesus promises that all of this will happen if we will simply abide in Him and let His words abide in us.

The other aspect of bearing fruit is helping others to come into an intimate relationship with the Father and the Son. Jesus said, "**But you will receive power when the Holy Spirit comes on you; and you will be my witnesses in Jerusalem, and in all Judea and Samaria, and to the ends of the earth**" (Acts 1:8).

9. The Father Wants to Bring About Justice on Your Behalf

When you were born again, you became a child of God (John 1:12). Jesus refers to you as one of God's chosen ones and plainly tells us that God will listen to your pleadings for justice when you are wronged by others. Although His timing may be different from yours, He will bring about justice in His way and in His time. Jesus said, "**And will not God bring about justice for his chosen ones, who cry out to him day and night? Will he keep putting them off? I tell you, he will see that they get justice, and quickly**" (Luke 18:7–8).

10. The Father Knows Your Needs and Wants to Meet Them

It's not uncommon for us to act as if God is a "Santa Claus God." We're tempted to think, He's got all the goodies (in heaven instead of the North Pole), and if we are good enough and do all the right things, avoid all of the wrong things, and pray and plead our case just right, He'll consider giving us what we need and maybe even give us what we want. That is not the Father Jesus reveals. He told us, "**So do not worry, saying, 'What shall we eat?' or 'What shall we drink?' or 'What shall we wear?' For the pagans run after all these things, and your heavenly Father knows that you need them. But seek first his kingdom and his righteousness, and all these things will be given to you as well**" (Matt. 6:31–33). When we are born of the Spirit (John 3), we become an adopted child of God. He is our heavenly Father. He's already proved His love by sending us the Good Shepherd to rescue us and lead us. He's already saved us with the finished atoning sacrifice of His dear Son. And in the previous verse Jesus tells us that the Father knows our needs to the finest details and wants to provide the care we need by meeting those needs. Jesus tells us that we don't have to beg the Father to meet our needs, and we don't even have to use a lot of words over and over again to plead for our needs. He said, "**And when you pray, do not keep on babbling like pagans, for they think they will be heard because of their many words. Do not be like them, for your Father knows what you need before you ask him**" (Matt. 6:7–8).

You may say, "Since the Father knows my needs before I ask for them, why pray and ask at all?" The answer is He wants fellowship with you, and fellowship requires honest, two-way communication. For example, you may know of something that your children really want. But even though you know what they want, hearing them tell you what they need or want creates a greater bond and intimacy. That's what honest and transparent prayer creates between us and the Father.

At the same time, He wants you to hear His heart and mind. And that's why we must meditate on Jesus' words—because He has already communicated everything the Father wants us to hear. And if we meditate on Jesus words, the Holy Spirit is able to perform His ministry of instantly bringing to mind Jesus' perfect words for the moment we are in (John 14:26).

11. The Father Wants You to Ask, Seek, and Knock

Remember when your children were little and they would either hint or tell you what they wanted for Christmas? Whether they were sheepish in their approach or bold, did you ever resent it? Of course not. I was always delighted, whether they would just hint around or whether they would come right out and tell me. I loved listening to their requests because they were communicating their hearts.

Remember when you were a child and wanted Santa and your parents to know what you really wanted? My sister was always a little shy about asking, but not me. I was never afraid to ask. My parents would listen, but they would never say yes or no.

I've also always loved when my children or grandchildren come up to me and ask questions. Whether they want an answer or just want to know what I thought or how I felt about something, it always feels great when they ask. I loved it when my kids were young, and I love it just as much now that they're adults. It truly fills my heart with joy. When they ask, it shows that they value my knowledge, experience, thoughts, and opinions, and I feel honored. And I'm always delighted to see their eyes and smiles and other responses when I answer them.

Jesus tells us that this is even truer with our heavenly Father. He revealed this about our relationship with the Father when He said, "Ask and it will be given to you; seek and you will find; knock and **the door will be opened to you. For everyone who asks receives; the one who seeks finds; and to the one who knocks, the door will be opened**" (Matt. 7:7–8). In this passage, Jesus is talking about our asking the Father for the things or information that we desire, seeking from the Father His wisdom about anything we are considering doing, and knocking on the Father's door to invite His help and guidance. Jesus completes this thought by saying, "**Which of you, if your son asks for bread, will give him a stone? Or if he asks for a fish, will give him a snake? If you, then, though you are evil, know how to give good gifts to your children, how much more will your Father in heaven give good gifts to those who ask him!**" (vv. 9–11). Once again Jesus is telling us that God really is our heavenly Father and wants to provide us with everything that is truly in our best interest. He doesn't hide from us. He doesn't avoid us. He wants to participate in every aspect of our journey through this life.

12. The Father Wants You to Experience a Joy That Fills Your Heart and Overflows to Others

When it comes to happiness, there are really two types: circumstantial happiness and spiritual joy. Both are wonderful, but only one is permanent. Circumstantial happiness is a happiness that is produced by the positive circumstances that come our way. It can elevate our feelings to the highest mountaintops—and when the circumstances producing that happiness are altered or even removed from our lives, it can take us into the darkest nights and the depths of despair. That is simply the nature of circumstantial happiness, and it tends to be the primary focus and desire of our human nature. There's nothing wrong with circumstantial happiness—we all love it and we all embrace it. We love when it takes us to the heights, and we hate it when it drives us to the depths.

But God wants to give us a spiritual joy that is not based on circumstances. Not only does He want to give us this joy—He wants to give it to us abundantly. He wants to fill our hearts with this joy to the point of overflowing—spilling out of our hearts and affecting those who surround us and those who enter our path for even a moment. This is the kind of joy Jesus had, and He even referred to it as "**My joy.**" In John 15, Jesus told the disciples and us some things that He promised would put His joy in us. He said, "**These things I have spoken to you so that My joy may be in you, and that your joy may be made full**" (v. 11 NASB).

His timing truly reflects how amazing is His love and care for His disciples and for us. You see, He was only a matter of minutes from being arrested, abused, mocked, beaten, mercilessly whipped, and crucified. He knew all of this was no more than an hour away. Yet His focus wasn't on the horrors He was about to experience. His focus was on telling His disciples how they could receive His joy and that His joy would fill their hearts with joy.

If you knew that you were about to be arrested, stripped, beaten, mocked, whipped, and nailed to a cross, do you think you would have any joy at all? Would you be so concerned about your children's future grieving that you would take time to tell them how you will give them your joy, and that your joy will be so powerful it will fill their hearts and keep them filled to the brim with joy? That's what Jesus was doing here. His joy is not subject to circumstances. Its source and its ability to fill our hearts is not connected in any way to circumstances and is not altered by even the worst of those circumstances. Of course, horrible circumstances can temporarily blind us to this joy and can even temporarily shove it into a closet in the back of our minds— but they cannot drain even a drop of this joy from our spirit. That's because God the Father and Jesus and the Holy Spirit are the source of that joy.

Sadly, the disciples didn't receive this joy until the Holy Spirit filled their hearts on the day of Pentecost, forty days after Jesus' resurrection. The question is how we can receive Jesus' joy into our hearts. We don't have to guess the answer, because Jesus answered this question in this same chapter of John.

God's Joy for *You*

As we just read, Jesus said, "**These things I have spoken to you so that My joy may be in you, and that your joy may be made full.**" The question is, what did He mean by "these things"? Right before He revealed that His joy could be in us and fill us up, He revealed several other critical truths. He revealed to us that we cannot do anything of eternal worth apart from Him. We need to remain connected to Him just as branches are connected to a vine. He then told us that if we would abide (remain) in Him, and if His words would abide in us, our prayers would be answered and we would bear much fruit and thus glorify the Father. Then, right before Jesus talked about His joy, He told us that He has loved us in the same way and to the same degree that the Father has loved Him. Then, immediately before He voiced "these things," He said, "**Abide in my love. If you keep my commandments, you will abide in my love, just as I have kept my Father's commandments and abide in his love**" (John 15:9–10 ESV). The way to receive Jesus' amazing joy is to abide (continually dwell) within His love, just like He continually dwells in His Father's love. How do we do that? The same way He did. He continually dwelt in the Father's love by obeying the Father's commands, and so we are to continually dwell in Jesus' love by obeying His commands. Remember, Jesus' commands don't weigh us down or burden us but rather empower us to grow our faith and love Him and the Father the way They want to be loved.

How amazing is this? When we use Their love language, not only do They bring us into intimacy (John 14:21–23), but it enables us to reside in the center of God's love and fills us with Jesus' joy. He then tells us that when we have His joy, no one (and no circumstance) will be able to take it away from us. He doesn't promise us a life free from heartache and grief. To the contrary, He tells us we will have troubles, heartaches, and griefs. He said, "**Very truly I tell you, you will weep and mourn while the world rejoices. You will grieve, but your grief will turn to joy. A woman** giving birth to a child has pain because her time has come; but when her baby is born she forgets the anguish because of her joy that a child is born into the world. So with you: Now is your time of grief, but I will see you again and you will rejoice, and no one will take away your joy" (John 16:20–22). He then went on to say, "I have told you these things, so that in me you may have peace. In this world you will have trouble. But take heart! I have overcome the world" (v. 33). These same things He told us in John, which will enable us to experience His joy, will also give us a supernatural peace that the world can't explain. A peace that filled His heart from the time He left Gethsemane until the moment He joyfully proclaimed, "It is finished" (John 19:30). This is His unshakable joy and His immovable peace, and it's ours when we love Him and the Father with Their love language.

As we have seen in the chapters of this book, these are just a few of Jesus' more than one hundred statements that reveal the truth about the Father. But Jesus not only revealed the Father in His statements; He revealed Him with His life. As we saw previously, at the Last Supper Jesus told His disciples, "Anyone who has seen me has seen the Father. . . . The words I say to you I do not speak on my own authority. Rather, it is the Father, living in me, who is doing his work. Believe me when I say that I am in the Father and the Father is in me; or at least believe on the evidence of the works themselves" (John 14:9–11).

Jesus' union with the Father was so absolute, so perfect that He did exactly what pleased the Father. Here, Jesus is telling us that you can look at anything and everything He said and did, and you can correctly assume that you are seeing and hearing the Father in Jesus' behavior and words. Knowing this, you can look at any event in Jesus' life, any inter-action with others, any attitude, and you can say, "I'm watching Jesus do precisely what the Father would do in that situation."

When you read about Jesus with the woman at the well, you're learning how the Father would react in that same situation. You can read about the Father in Jesus' interactions with the rich young ruler, the ten lepers, Zacchaeus, Mary and Martha, the disciples in the storm, and on and on. This is one more reason to read through every situation in Jesus' life and every passage in the four gospels—so you can see and hear the Father and the Son. As you do, you will get to know Them, and to know Them is to love Them.

If you don't know where to start, I would start in the Gospel of John. As you do, you will witness God in ways that neither Joseph nor David nor even the prophets had the opportunity to see. Jesus said, **"For I tell you that many prophets and kings desired to see what you see, and did not see it, and to hear what you hear, and did not hear it"** (Luke 10:24 ESV). Don't let this glorious opportunity pass you by. Get serious, and focus on the life and teachings of the Lord of lords and King of kings.

THE JOSEPH PRINCIPLES

Joseph Principle #1
Seeing How Every Trial Produces
Hidden Treasures

Joseph Principle #2
Knowing and Experiencing the
Intimate Presence of God

Joseph Principle #3
Believing That God Is Sovereign and
Loving and Living That Belief

Joseph Principle #4
Living in the Moment with God and Others

Joseph Principle #5
Listening to the Whispers of God

Joseph Principle #6
Expecting God to Work His
Miracles Through Your Faith

Joseph Principle #7
Forgiving Others Because God Forgives Us

Joseph Principle #8
Accelerating Achievement with a
Vision, a Plan, and a Schedule

Joseph Principle #9
Allowing One Vision to Die So a
Better Vision May Be Born

Joseph Principle #10
Dethroning Grief from God's
Throne in Your Heart

Joseph Principle #11
Gaining a True Vision of the True God

Joseph Principle #12
Yielding Your Perceived Rights to God

ADDITIONAL EXAMPLE
OF THE VISION
MAPPING PROCESS

Vision Statement: Create a television commercial campaign for NeumiSkin Topical Skin Care Spray

Goals

1. Recruit a celebrity endorser
2. Write spots—30-second spot, 60-second spot, 120-second spot
3. Select before and after photos
4. Select media company to purchase test campaign and roll-out campaign
5. Select dates for test campaign and for roll-out campaign
6. Shoot commercials

Intermediate Steps for Each Goal

1. Recruit a celebrity endorser
   a. Create wish list of celebrities
   b. Check Q scores on each celebrity

    c. Prioritize list

    d. Write pitch for top three names on list

    e. Call agent

    f. Meet with celeb

2. Write spots

    a. Identify product benefits and prioritize

    b. Identify product features and prioritize

    c. Create hooks and prioritize

    d. Determine word pictures

    e. Determine offer

    f. Write initial drafts

    g. Read to beta group

3. Select before and after photos

    a. Review current photos

    b. Ask for submissions from our distributors in Australia, New Zealand, and Latin America

    c. Make selections

4. Select media company to purchase test campaign and roll-out campaign

    a. Meet with ATC group

    b. Meet with Ken T.

5. Select dates

    a. Set test campaign and roll-out campaign dates

    b. Confirm celeb availability dates

6. Shoot commercials

    a. Scout and select locations

    b. Cast extras

    c. Select testimonials

    d. Select experts

    e. Assign shooting dates

NOTES

Introduction

1. "10 Leading Causes of Death by Age Group, United States—2018," National Vital Statistics System, National Center for Health Statistics, CDC, https://www.cdc.gov/injury/wisqars/pdf/leading_causes_of_death _by_age_group_2018-508.pdf.
2. Martha Lally and Suzanne Valentine-French, "Grief: Loss of Children and Parents," *Lifespan Development: A Psychological Perspective*, no. 2. https:// courses.lumenlearning.com/suny-lifespandevelopment/chapter/grief-loss -of-children-and-parents.

Chapter 1

1. Scott Reyburn, "Cimabue Painting Discovered in French Kitchen Fetches Nearly $27 Million," *New York Times*, October 27, 2019, https://www .nytimes.com/2019/10/27/arts/design/cimabue-painting-auction.html.
2. Benji, "How Long Does a Diamond Take to Form?," Leibish, June 21, 2017, https://www.leibish.com/how-long-does-a-diamond-take-to-form-article -1447.

Chapter 3

1. James Robison, "My 55-Year Journey Following Jesus (Part 1)," blog, July 17, 2014, https://jamesrobison.net/my-55-year-journey-following -jesus-part-1.
2. James Robison, "My Journey (Part 2)," blog, July 24, 2014, https:// jamesrobison.net/my-journey-2.
3. Robison, "My Journey (Part 2)."
4. "About the Author," blog, https://jamesrobison.net/about/.

Chapter 4

1. Matthew A. Killingsworth and Daniel T. Gilbert, "A Wandering Mind Is an Unhappy Mind," *Science* 330, no. 6006 (November 12, 2010): 93, https://wjh-www.harvard.edu/~dtg/KILLINGSWORTH%20&%20 GILBERT%20(2010).pdf.
2. Harvard University, "Mind Is a Frequent, but Not Happy, Wanderer: People Spend Nearly Half Their Waking Hours Thinking About What Isn't Going on Around Them," ScienceDaily, November 12, 2010, www .sciencedaily.com/releases/2010/11/101111141759.htm.

Chapter 6

1. Steven K. Scott, *The Greatest Words Ever Spoken: Everything Jesus Said About You, Your Life, and Everything Else* (Colorado Springs: WaterBrook, 2010), 206–16.
2. Scott, *Greatest Words Ever Spoken*, 298–304.
3. Scott, *Greatest Words Ever Spoken*.

Chapter 8

1. C. S. Lewis, *Mere Christianity* (San Francisco: HarperOne, 2015), 115.
2. C. S. Lewis, *The Weight of Glory* (San Francisco: HarperOne, 2015), 178.
3. Jud Davis, "God 10,000 Talents and Forgiving a Sinning Brother," *Dayton (TN) Herald-News*, November 3, 2015, https://www.rheaheraldnews.com /lifestyles/article_334f283e-8262-11e5-aaf7-53cf9a2b76bb.html.
4. Some of the emotions God feels include love (Jer. 31:3) and joy (Isa. 62:5; Jer. 32:41; Zeph. 3:17). He feels grief (Gen. 6:6; Ps. 78:40), and He also laughs (Ps. 2:4, 37:13; Prov. 1:26). His heart is moved by compassion (Deut. 32:36; Judg. 2:18; Ps. 135:14).

Chapter 11

1. Martha Lally and Suzanne Valentine-French, "Grief: Loss of Children and Parents," *Lifespan Development: A Psychological Perspective,* no. 2, https:// courses.lumenlearning.com/suny-lifespandevelopment/chapter/grief-loss -of-children-and-parents.
2. "Grief Can Hurt—in More Ways than One," Harvard Health Publishing, February 1, 2019, https://www.health.harvard.edu/mind-and-mood/grief -can-hurt-in-more-ways-than-one.

3. W. E. Vine, *Vine's Expository Dictionary of Old and New Testament Words* (Nashville: Thomas Nelson, 2003).

4. Nick Vujicic, *Life Without Limits: Inspiration for a Ridiculously Good Life* (Colorado Springs: WaterBrook, 2012).

ACKNOWLEDGMENTS

Shannon—You are defined by kindness, compassion, and generosity. Your life, your Christlike heart, and your treatment of others (even strangers) are never-ending examples of how Jesus wants *me* to be. I envy your childlike faith and love for our heavenly Father and His dear Son. You are truly a bright and shining beacon to me and to everyone who crosses your path.

Gary Smalley—My brother, my best friend, my mentor. Though I haven't heard your voice for six years, your words and teachings echo in my mind and continue to bless my life and ministry every day. A day never passes that I don't think of you. Even though you're gone, you *still* make me smile and laugh out loud.

Jim and Patty Shaughnessy, and Tom and Marlene Delnoce—My lifetime best friends who have always been there for me in good times and bad; I can't imagine my life without your presence and wonderful influence and support.

Herb and Helen Selby, and Wayne and Mary Shuart—My spiritual parents from the beginning of my life with Christ. Fifty-eight years of love, kindness, encouragement, and living examples of what it means to love and follow Jesus. I'm so very grateful.

My sweet sister, Sandy Heinze—Where would I be if you hadn't loved me and taken me to that glorious place where I came to know Christ?

Jan Miller—For twenty-seven years you have represented me and my books in a way that few authors have ever been represented. I'm sure I'm at the bottom of your amazing list of bestselling authors, yet the love, kindness, and wisdom you have given to me and each of my projects has made me feel like I'm at the top. Jan, you are truly in a league of your own. I am so honored to be included in your stable of authors. Even more, I am so grateful for your love and friendship.

Pastor Ron Johnson and Sandy—Thank you for your wonderful friendship and faithful ministry to me, our family, and our companies.

Pastor Troy Champ—Every Sunday you stir my heart and make me want to love and follow Jesus more intensely.

Kyle Olund—I'm so grateful for you, your vision, and your commitment to *our* book. Thanks, Kyle.

Whitney Bak, Leslie Peterson, Lauren Bridges—My supercalifragilisticexpialidocious editors! All of your work on our manuscript was truly extraordinary. Thank you so very much.

ABOUT THE AUTHOR

Steven K. Scott is the bestselling author of *The Richest Man Who Ever Lived, Mentored by a Millionaire, Simple Steps to Impossible Dreams,* and *The Greatest Words Ever Spoken.* Scott is the cofounder of the American Telecast Corporation, Total Gym Fitness, and Neumi. Scott is a popular international speaker on the subjects of personal and professional achievement and the application of biblical wisdom and Jesus' teachings to every area of life.